A Creed for Free Enterprise

A Creed for
Free Enterprise

by
CLARENCE B. RANDALL

An Atlantic Monthly Press Book
Little, Brown and Company · Boston

ATLANTIC–LITTLE, BROWN BOOKS
ARE PUBLISHED BY
LITTLE, BROWN AND COMPANY
IN ASSOCIATION WITH
THE ATLANTIC MONTHLY PRESS

*Published simultaneously
in Canada by McClelland and Stewart Limited*

PRINTED IN THE UNITED STATES OF AMERICA

Contents

A Creed for Free Enterprise

CHAPTER I A Time to Speak

I AM as much surprised as my friends will be to find that I have written a book. Until now my hallmark has been an off-the-cuff talk at a businessman's luncheon or dinner, done in the spirit of the occasion and without manuscript. It has been my habit merely to stand up and say what I think, as though I were talking to a group of associates in my office, letting the words come as best they might. In so doing, I have tried to demonstrate by example that businessmen can and should stand up and say what they think whenever people will listen.

I now try to carry that one step further. I believe that we should also address ourselves to the reading public, that vast company of thoughtful citizens who are not invited to our luncheons, and who do not know us. I am convinced that businessmen must write as well as speak, in order that we may bring to people everywhere the exciting and confident message of our faith in the free enterprise way of life.

We are not doing that now. We have learned how to use every modern tool except language, yet that is the tool our enemies use best. We believe in our hearts that the individualistic philosophy of social organization brings greater happiness to more people than the collectivist, but we seldom say so, and when we do, we say it only to ourselves.

This is the age of ideas. Facts and machines are still wondrously important, but it is what men believe that controls the world we live in, and what men think that threatens our way of life. The battle of ideologies is on, and we could lose it by default. If a great fire were raging in one of our plants, every man who could get there would drop whatever he was doing, no matter how important it seemed, and rush to lend a hand. Anything to save the plant! That sort of emergency compels action because you can see it; fire crackles, walls tumble in, and smoke chokes your throat.

But the glibness of the socialist planner, which rings so falsely in our ears, is a new phenomenon for which we are not psychologically prepared, and we wait timidly for others to provide the answers instead of vigorously proclaiming the truth as we ourselves see it.

Take the colleges, for example. We are critical that the American enterprise system is not taught in forthright fashion to the eager minds of the postwar student groups. But the faculties reply that there are no books on business written by businessmen to put on the shelves of their libraries. They rather reasonably ask why if we hold such deep convictions we do not put them in writing.

What a change would come in this struggle for men's minds if suddenly there could pour out from the world of American business a torrent of intelligent, forward-looking thinking, flowing straight from the hearts of thousands of the fine men who lead our institutions, that would tell not only the miracle of production, but the hopes and aspirations for a better world which I know these men actually to hold. The mass impact for good of that leadership would be irresistible.

But we can't do it by silence. If we are today misunderstood and undervalued by the American public, it is we ourselves who are at fault. It is not the fault of the way of life we represent. Actually the free enterprise method of production, carried on within the political climate of democratic freedom, is the social system which has brought the highest degree of welfare to the most people. We know that, but can't say it. Our public is told about business by professors and commentators and politicians and preachers and labor leaders, but seldom by the men who know most about it, the businessmen themselves.

Psychologically, however, my generation of management men has one severe handicap to overcome in achieving public leadership. Our approach to social questions is apt to be negative. Our habit of thought is to be against things, and we have little skill in creating concepts that other people will be for. We have raised invective to a fine art, but developed little capacity for throwing on the screen of our national consciousness pictures that evoke enthusiasm and admiration. With brick and mortar and stainless steel we are the greatest builders the world has ever seen, but our daring and confidence seem to leave us when we walk out of the plant into the realm of ideas.

It will not be easy, therefore, for us as individuals to form a clear pattern of thinking in our own minds that will be positive in its bearing on the problems, and that will cause others to warm toward us. Thinking takes time, and isn't always pleasant. To shut the office door, put your feet up, and look out the window seems somehow to be letting the stockholders down. We easily convince ourselves that we are making great efforts when we measure ourselves by the number of engagements we keep, people we see, and reports we read, but, actually, the thing business needs most today is an occasional quiet hour for the boss. To reflect before doing may be more important than the doing, but as executives we are much happier doing than reflecting.

And then, of course, we greatly need freshness and individuality in our thinking. We are victims of the same pattern-mindedness that we decry in the mass movements.

Individuality means being ourselves. To that end, I early decided that I would not show the manuscript of this book to my business associates until it had been published. What I shall say is not to be considered in any way a statement of the views of Inland Steel Company, nor of our management staff. My colleagues have their own individual views, and their own ways of expressing them. What I am saying are the convictions of but one man. Too often these days when an executive attempts a speech and it turns out to be the old familiar eye-wash, it is because the manuscript was widely circulated and was watered down by everyone who saw it. The lawyers, the sales department, the industrial relations people, the public relations director, they all had a shot at it, and only the platitudes were left. Words are persuasive when they are the heart throbs of an individual, and a speech or a book to be effective must mirror the man.

Let's assume, then, that the businessman knows what he believes, that he has informed himself competently as to contemporary problems in his own community and the country at large, has many times set aside a quiet hour for heart searching, has formed clear opinions, and established in his own life a personal philosophy that really motivates his conduct. Why, then, is he inept in expressing himself? Why does he duck going over to his local high school to speak before the student assembly? Why would he feel silly if invited to address a convention of the League of Women Voters? Why does he send his lawyer to appear before a Congressional committee instead of going down himself? Why, when past middle life his big chance comes and he rises before a really great audience to whom his name is a by-word for so-called success, does he hold with trembling fingers the speech written for him by a hired hand who can't possibly have insight like that born of his own wide experience, and give the game away by stumbling over the pronunciation of unaccustomed words? We all know the signs of the ghost-written speech, the folksy gaiety that isn't his, the classical allusions from books we know he hasn't read, and the punch line that he couldn't possibly have thought up. The audience feels let down, and goes home convinced that they were right all the time in thinking that big businessmen aren't much. They came to hear him, and heard someone else. They would much rather hear him say things badly, but with the integrity of his personality shining through those clumsy sentences, than listen to a fraud.

Yet that same man is positively eloquent on other occasions. Watch him when he calls on his best customer. The words simply pour from his lips, the right words, and with perfect timing, and just enough of them. Most assuredly he doesn't reach in his pocket for a piece of paper and start reading. He knows what he believes about his product, and he holds such deep convictions that the words form themselves instinctively. Why can't he be that way about free enterprise as a better way of life than socialism? There is vastly more at stake for him in that than in making the biggest sale he ever made, but for some reason the words won't come. Frankly I don't understand it. But I do know this: the next generation of businessmen will be articulate, knowing what they believe and entering joyously into the battle of ideas, or there

[9   ]

will be no business as we have known it heretofore.

But there is one further circumstance that might limit the impact of ideas flowing from the business world upon public opinion, and that is the personal standing of businessmen themselves in their own communities. People pay best attention to the words of those whom they most respect. I shall say more of this later, but the thought cannot be repeated too often. The businessman who has not established himself favorably in the affections of those about him, in ways disassociated from his business, is not a leader in that community, and no one will be much impressed by anything that he says on any subject. If he has proved himself worthy of their confidence when his business was not at issue, they will listen to him when he reasons with them about his business, but not otherwise. Our miracle of production is not enough of itself to perpetuate the system that made it possible. Ideas are created by people, and do not exist apart from people. Only proven leaders can perpetuate them.

So much as to why I wrote a book. Now for the book itself. I have tried to practice what I am preaching, and have tried to say what I believe. I have done it with great inner trepidation. As a friend of mine would say, "I have put on my hair shirt." I can only hope that as those who are kind enough to read these lines may differ either in principle or as to my mode of expression, they themselves will give voice to their dissent, thus widening the area of discussion and stimulating once again the American habit of debate, from whence has come our wisdom in the past.

CHAPTER II Production: Tool of
Society

OBVIOUSLY, the first task to which the businessman
must set himself upon trying to clarify his thinking
is an understanding and proper evaluation of free
enterprise itself. Here we seem to be on familiar
ground. Free enterprise is our favorite theme on those
rare occasions when we talk; no banquet would be
complete without sonorous phrases in its praise, our
advertisements proclaim it by word and picture; yet,
actually, who among us so comprehends its significance
that he can persuade an honest skeptic of its virtues?
So often we argue only by declaration and vitupera-
tion, striving to beat down the opposition solely by
the noise our voices make, without sensing that no
one is listening. We do, however, thus reveal the
shallowness of our understanding, and strengthen the
suspicion of the public that our fervor is based
solely on a selfish desire to preserve the status quo

in which we are thought to be a privileged class.

Yet our record of performance is magnificent. One has only to look about in the rest of the world today to perceive that there is something very different about the economic well-being of the fortunate citizens of the United States, and that it is a difference which has saved what there is of freedom for all mankind. In two wars the American system of production has been the anchor of the free world, and today it is the sole effective deterrent to further aggression. Without it all would have been lost. Shall that lesson be lightly ignored? Shall the sneering contempt of a small group of cosmic experimenters be allowed to destroy what so many millions of men have toiled to create since the earliest days of our Republic? Every businessman in the country cries out daily for a champion who will nail these monstrous lies being put out by the enemies of his beloved free enterprise, but as for his own part in the counter crusade it sometimes turns out that "he is tied up at the moment, trying to straighten out his production schedule for the next quarter," and besides it is very hard for him to write speeches.

And therein lies our problem. No one man can do this job. And no one can be hired to do it for us. But if each man who is a part of free enterprise would come to hold the deep conviction that the perpetuation of the system itself had first priority on his talents, and if every such voice could be lifted all of the time in humble and intelligent exposition of the values of the system as the man sees them, public opinion would have to come our way overnight for the simple reason that the things we believe in are just and right. Only misunderstanding is in the way.

These things seem so clear to us that again one asks why it is that we do so badly.

First of all, curiously enough, we bog down in semantics. We, of all people, ought not to quibble over words, but we do. We quarrel with one another as to whether "free enterprise" is both complete and accurate as a description of the business system whose virtues we wish to praise. Many a monograph has been written on that subject, and much ingenuity has been employed to devise improved phrases, but I notice that none gets currency beyond that given it by the man who was the inventor. The same thing happens as to the word "democracy." Often when I have used the word "democracy" in a public address I have had to face at the close an angry citizen who has paid no attention to the substance of my argument because he has been so determined to convert me to the idea that we live in a republic. And I have a friend who simply froths at the mouth when I use the word "worker" instead of "employee" or "fellow-worker" because, he says, even the president of a company is a worker. I am impatient of these minutiae. A general audience hearing those words is not confused. Hair-splitting annoys them: they want to know what businessmen are going to do about those things. And so I say that when we contrast the proven values of free enterprise with the proven failure of socialism people know what we are talking about.

Apart from these rather sophomoric semantics, I suppose that our first and perhaps our most fundamental failure to understand the real meaning of free enterprise is to consider it synonymous with production. How we love to boast about production. I do myself. Take the steel industry, for example. In other wars, we were asked simply to divert our output from peacetime needs to armament, but when war came in Korea the new challenge was that we should carry the full normal civilian demand and yet superimpose upon that the greatest rearmament load the country has ever attempted. And in spite of the vast new capital which this required, and physical problems which taxed our resources to the limit, we have done just that. Who

[15]

wouldn't be proud of such a record? And all over the country in all the great industries and in thousands of plants, both large and small, men are bursting with similar pride at the breaking of production records.

But our strength is our weakness. We have come to worship production as an end in itself, which of course it is not. We have come to give production a place of distorted importance in the scale of human values, as though it settled every question and answered every need. It is precisely there that the honest critic of our way of life makes his attack, and finds us vulnerable.

Production, as I see it, is merely a tool to be used by society for its own advancement. To produce more and more with less and less effort is merely treading water unless we thereby release time and energy for the cultivation of the mind and spirit, and the achievement of those ends for which Providence placed us on this earth. Surely there must be for each person some ultimate value, some purpose, some mode of self-expression that makes the experience we call life richer and deeper. How forlorn it would all be otherwise. Taken collectively, the diligent and honest pursuit of those values by all thoughtful men makes the world a better place, and mankind progresses. Better production does not in itself accomplish those ends. It merely gives us more time for trying.

But with our American capacity for production thus set in its proper perspective, it justifiably stands out as a phenomenon for all the world to admire, and for us to re-examine critically in order that once fully understood the secret formula may never be lost by neglect or abandoned by default. The key to it obviously is the intelligent harnessing of the self-interest of the individual for the advancement of the common good. Throughout the countless ages that lie buried in the past, those species survived and improved in which each individual concentrated on taking care of himself. That instinct, as a force in human behavior, has eons of momentum behind it. Our wisdom lies in using it to promote the general welfare, while the fallacy of the collectivist dictator is his naive belief that it can or should be eliminated from human conduct.

However society may be organized in the political sense, the function of production remains the same. In Russia, as in the United States, the goal is the turning out of the maximum of goods and services with the minimum of time and labor in order that there may be a surplus of human effort that can be devoted to other ends. Every man must therefore be held to his task.

Slave states all through the centuries have done this by the whip. Russia has added modern refinements such as blackmail, but her system is still that of the strong compelling the weak by force to work. Her industrial relations problems must obviously center around indifference, sullenness, and sabotage. In sharp contrast to this, we base our industrial philosophy upon the effectiveness of the happy man. We work hard because we work for ourselves, a primordial urge that is as much a part of our being as eating food.

Most of the occasional nonsense written in this country to decry the profit motive is either ignorance or hypocrisy: it either is failure to understand the importance of self-interest in increasing the total wealth of all of the people, or just plain shutting of the eyes to the truth. For myself, I have never known a man who did not at times seek to advance his own self-interest. Professors, even those who attack our business system, vie keenly for better and bigger salaries, and clergymen want larger churches and better pay, all of which I consider to be normal and proper. Even a repulsively selfish man who knows no god but money may make tremendous contributions to society if his avarice causes him to bring into being a new or better product or produce an old one at a lower price. Just as many a necessary and useful structure may lack beauty, so may an unlovely person be useful to society. A horse with a very evil disposition can nevertheless pull the farmer's plow. So the secret of free enterprise is that we harness the natural instinct of each man to serve himself, and rely on other natural forces to see that as he serves himself he serves society.

Foremost among these forces is competition. In the management of a business the sharp bite of honest, aggressive competition is the automatic corrective that safeguards the public from extortion. No man can be said to be making too much profit if many others are trying to beat him at his own game and none can succeed. The larger his profit, the greater will be the number of those who will try and the greater the chance that they will succeed. Those who pursue him hotly have many points of attack — quality, design, service, and above all price — and he redoubles his effort as they approach because he knows that today's profit may be tomorrow's loss. He is spurred both by hope of gain and fear of loss, and never for a moment can he relax his effort. He spends his life actually producing the most that he can for the common good. How could there be a better formula than that for bringing about continuously the maximum of effort by all of the people? How can it be possible that in the long run the collective effort of nations ruled by force, where each member of society goes to his task reluctantly and without hope, will match that of free men going joyously about their tasks because they are permitted to help themselves as they add to the total wealth?

But it all hinges on the operation of the free market. No modern nation in this socially conscious world will long permit selfishness to go unrestrained, and if it is not held in check by competition because the free market has been interfered with, the people will assert themselves and take away the privileges of free enterprise by collective action. In the steel industry that means nationalization. In other words, the free market as created by honest competition is an indispensable part of the free enterprise system, and if as businessmen we desire to perpetuate the privileges we must accept with full integrity the correlative obligations and responsibilities. We will not be permitted to accept the one and reject the other. Free enterprise is not a hunting license. We must not exploit self-interest and at the same time handcuff the policeman whom society has established in the form of competition.

But not all American businessmen yet see this

clearly. There are still those who make the telephone call to their competitor before announcing a new price; still those who hesitate to enter a new market until their doing so has been cleared with the rest of the industry; still those who describe a trade association that quietly polices prices as "constructive." Such men have no business philosophy and no understanding of the way of life they seek to save. Daily they put expediency and short-term profit above principle and survival. Their conduct brings the whole system into disrepute, and it is high time that they learned that our public has never been so sensitive to lack of honesty as it is today. Curiously enough, such men are often naive to the point of denouncing government for suspending natural economic laws through the imposition of wage and price controls, although exercising privately themselves the right to suspend the free market. All that is needed is a little straight thinking and some old-fashioned character to put a stop to such practices; and they would stop overnight if we could make it clearly understood that free enterprise itself is at stake.

To document that statement, all that is required is to look overseas. With us our economy is still dynamic, creative, and vigorous; still bursting at the seams with new ideas, new products, and better methods; still displaying flashes of genius and breath-taking concepts; still daring to take great risks; still lighting the age-old fires of ambition in the eager minds of young men. But in Europe the economy is torpid and sick, kept alive for the most part by blood transfusions from the healthy arteries of our industry. Over there the young men seek security and have a depressing sense of fatalism about the future. They doubt whether there is anything they can do about themselves in particular or the world in general. Among the older businessmen are many who are very wise, and many who often seem to have a clearer understanding of the world in which they live than their counterparts among us, but there is a lack-lustre look in their eyes. They are defensive, sensitive to criticism, and more proud of what has been than of what is to be. Their spirit is not that of the risk-taking entrepreneur, but of the conservator of what their fathers and grandfathers have passed on to them.

These are, of course, generalizations, to which there are brilliant and heartening exceptions, as I should be the first to admit. The new Margam plant of the Steel Company of Wales, for example, is one of the finest steel-producing units in the world, admirably engineered and aggressively managed; the soon to be completed wide continuous sheet steel rolling mill of Sollac in the north of France will equal the best of ours in efficiency and will give light manufacturing in central Europe a tremendous stimulus; and few enterprises anywhere have more competent staff or more alert management than Holland's small but vigorous steel company. An American could learn much from any one of those operations. And when it came to shrewd world-wide merchandising he would do well to have a look at postwar Arbed in Luxemburg, the largest steel company in that interesting country and the largest company anywhere outside the United States.

But the characteristic of European businessmen as a class as distinguished from Americans is their complacency, their timidity, and their instinctive looking to each other and to government for protection against the rude shocks of the contemporary world. And the thing that they fear most is price competition. Almost to a man they are cartel-minded, and it seems to me to be a sound inference that their unwillingness to face honest, vigorous price competition is the cause of their technological backwardness. Their ingenuity has gone not into thinking up ways of beating their competition by lowering prices or entering new markets, but into ways of persuading their competitor that it would be unsocial for him to do either. And in this they have usually had the full support of their government. It is no coincidence, therefore, in my opinion, that those countries which are now turning to the United States for so-called technical assistance are those in which there have been no traditions of real competition and no laws against restraint of trade and monopolistic practices worthy of the name. And much as I admire many of the present leaders of the British steel industry, I am bound to say that in my opinion their rejection of price competition, their instinct for collectivism, and their willingness to accept government control in exchange for the right to agree on prices laid the foundation upon which it was easy for a hostile government to carry out nationalization. All of which brings me back once more to the deep conviction that an honest free market is the very essence of free enterprise and that we cannot hope to deny the one and preserve the other.

But the businessman who is earnestly seeking to think through his own personal philosophy about free enterprise must go one step further and reflect upon the nature of freedom itself. I have always been unhappy at the suggestion that freedom can be expressed in the plural. Rather it seems to me it is a concept that is indivisible and sole. There are no "freedoms": there is simply freedom, and it runs as the breath of life through every phase of the American tradition. In fact, it is America.

Those daring spirits who conquered our wilderness and founded our cities and wrote our laws and began our businesses were men who broke away. No man would turn his back on the land of his fathers and the place of his birth unless he felt within himself a desire so great that it was simply irresistible. That common desire which our successive waves of immigrants from the older countries all felt was simply to live their own lives. They asked no security, and looked only to the strength of their arms and the keenness of their minds to meet their needs. But they had deep respect for each other, and assumed that their neighbors would behave as they did.

It was of such forebears that American free enterprise was born, and such is its spirit. We propose to drive as hard as we can toward our own ends but we know that we must stop short of injuring others or the whole scheme will have to be abandoned. We rely on the conscience of the individual to guide business conduct toward the general welfare. This is the responsibility side of freedom that distinguishes it from license. It is the democratic tradition because it is a self-imposed restraint instead of one that is external, as in the totalitarian states. But it is obviously subject to abuse by those who do not understand, or worse still, by that small but evil minority of men who understand and consciously ignore conscience. And in any state, when men abuse freedom there has to be law. Society has no other way of preserving itself from those who will not play the game. The proliferation of laws restricting freedom of action may be taken as an indication that more and more people either do not understand the social obligations of freedom, or lack the moral courage to do what they know is right. And when it is the business community at which the laws are aimed, it may be a sign that free enterprise is dying because it is not understood by those who practice it.

Whether or not this is a correct analysis of our business system is of little moment. But that each American businessman owes it to himself and to the system of which he is a part to make his own analysis would seem to be clear. It is a time for heart searching and action. The march toward socialism and nationalization is on. We who would reverse that trend must recognize that this is so, and then accept day-to-day responsibility for doing something about it. But for our acts to be effective, we must first have understanding.

CHAPTER III Unions Never Lose

In trying to think his way through the problems of the day, the businessman might just as well tackle the tough ones first and make up his mind what he thinks about labor unions. They are here to stay, and if he doesn't like them as they are he might as well face the fact that they knew what they wanted and got a lot of things done while he was still content to be profane and say he would have no truck with them; and that they are still ahead of him in knowing what they want and getting things done. This will go on until he makes up his mind as to what is good and what is bad about them, and accepts the good and resists the bad with might and main.

I have seen it all from the beginning. I was just the right age and in just the right spot, when the storm broke, to have the labor problem thrown at me without warning, and of course without training. There was one such man in every company, and I happened to be the one in mine. I went through that bloody period of organizing by violence, with its mass assaults on the gates, its goon commandos that ranged from town to town breaking heads and destroying property, and I have stood in a governor's office pleading for troops to protect the lives of innocent people. Never to this day have I been able to forgive those national figures in the labor movement who whipped up the fury of those mobs and let those brutal deeds be done without a single gesture of protest. After that I fought the battle of the lawyers, and spent my days in a welter of injunctions and appeals. And my sleeve would be heavy with service stripes if there were one for every mediation conference in which I have participated or every fact-finding board before which I have testified. So it is hard for me to be objective, but I try to be just that, for I know that bias never settled anything.

The ideal attitude, for example, of an employer toward the union question can be stated quite simply, I think. The choice of whether to join or not to join a union should lie strictly with the individual worker. It is a matter to be determined within the confines of his own conscience. If he feels powerless as an individual in the face of the economic power possessed by his company, it is altogether understandable that he will want to associate himself with other like-minded men for mutual protection by joining a union. If that is his free choice the employer should accept it with complete integrity. That is the law, and it is also good industrial morals.

Such is the peaceful scene as commonly imagined by those well-meaning people who call every manufacturer a reactionary, but unhappily it isn't usually that simple. A good employer knows his men; they talk to him privately and he feels that they speak the truth. When they tell him that they distrust the union organizers, that they believe them to be both dishonest and unpatriotic, but that they are sure they will have two feet of cold gas pipe laid across their ears if they don't sign up, the management man goes hot with anger because he feels deep sympathy for the dilemma of his men. I have heard labor leaders publicly defend such violence on the ground that their cause advances social justice and that no individual has the right to stand in the way. I have heard them say publicly that they would refuse to obey a court injunction that forbade violence. And, since I consider respect for law and order and the rights of minorities to be fundamental in this land of the free, I repeat that I find it hard to be objective.

The modern statutes have assuaged this somewhat, and the secret ballot under public auspices gets at the truth of what the employee really wants. I have no sympathy for the employer who ignores that truth. If his men really want a union, he has but one honest course, to accept the verdict and enter into the new relationship with a sincere determination to make it work.

But the well-meaning intellectual will be far off the mark if he thinks that the new laws have brought full democracy to the internal administration of labor unions. Reflect, for example, upon the lack of turn-over in the men who hold the top offices in the nation-wide unions. There is no security like it in the world, and no parallel for it in any other situation where men are chosen by popular ballot. The same names have been before us for a generation. Reflect also upon their lush expense accounts, their Cadillacs, their vacations in Florida, and their year-round suites in the best hotels. And when, if ever, does the elaborate window dressing of a national policy conference result in a rousing vote to turn down the program brought forth from the inner circle?

Even in the locals there is very little genuine grass roots thinking. A union in a large plant that might have 10,000 members seldom has 400 at a meeting, and the inner circle runs the show. The thoughtful worker who doesn't want to strike stays away from the meeting, for it isn't healthy to be labeled a management stooge. The indifference of voters to the great issues in a national election is as nothing when compared to the apathy of the great mass of union members toward the inner politics of their union. Indifference, however, is probably the wrong word. It is more a sense of complete futility.

When we turn away from this question of how far the individual member of a local union is coerced by a small inside group, which after all is a matter that the worker can straighten out for himself if he will go about it, and turn to ask how far the American people as a whole have been coerced by big labor, there can be no two opinions. "Clear it with Sidney" has become a national policy. With a skill and perseverance that one must respect if not admire, a few men who represent but one segment of the nation have achieved for themselves a power over the welfare of all such as no elected public official has ever held or ever could hold constitutionally.

Never for a moment does the pressure relax. No national emergency has been so severe but that it has been used for their advantage, and no ultimate objective has ever been suggested which, if accomplished, would end the pressure. Power is the thing, power exercised for some against the rest. People often ask me what it is that organized labor really wants, and I have to reply sadly that there is no final concession which if granted by management would end the strife. A great labor leader who announced that he had reached the final goal would be thrown out and replaced by the man who promised more, and so to keep himself in office he must and does go on forever promising more. But management cannot go on forever giving more. In the broad sense the men who manage a business are merely the agents of the public. It is the public really who give, and soon there will be nothing more to give. So I say that there come times when management simply must say no to big labor and make it stick.

What are the manifestations of this power?

First, the casting of all American life into a pattern, the settling down of a deadly sameness over institutions and people everywhere with resultant lessening of the worth of the individual and resistance to variation; the "we know better than you what is good for you" approach to the problems of individual Americans, precisely as though we were on our way toward the dictatorship of the proletariat — which we may be, for all I know.

Industry-wide bargaining is one of the whips by which we are marched toward this strangely un-American pattern type of existence in industry. We goose-step to the music of Pittsburgh. If one steel company, having in mind only its own circumstances and needs, arrives fairly at a bargain with its workers, forthwith it is decreed that this shall be the pattern, and that six hundred other companies, large and small, located in widely separated geographical areas, and having heaven knows what circumstances and what needs, shall sign on the dotted line. Try as they may, they will not be permitted to reopen the discussion, even though the contract may destroy the company. They will be told by the so-called international representative of the union that he has no authority to grant concessions, this at the same time that the members of the local are being told that the management is not bargaining in good faith.

To be quite fair I must admit that this is not true of all labor leaders: from time to time one encounters at the local and district levels in union organizations representatives who display an independence that is most heartening, and that gives one hope that perhaps eventually better relationships will prevail. I have seen a man stand up to his international officers courageously, and at the risk of his job defend the position of the employer because he believed it to be right. And I have seen the same man stand up to his boss and tell him off too, when he believed him to be wrong. That sort of conduct will advance labor peace.

I wish that I might now leave the point of nationwide patterns and not display the reverse side of the shield, but because I am trying to show how important it seems to me to be for each businessman to relate the consequences of his own acts to the preservation of free enterprise, there are certain things that need saying. The truth is that occasionally we have been given a long shove down this path toward the supreme pattern of nation-wide sameness by management itself. Not only during the war did some industrial leaders openly advocate industry-wide bargaining, but then and now many more have accepted it with a smirk of complacency. They like the security of knowing precisely what their competitors' labor costs will be, and so long as the good times last and they can pass the burden on to the public through higher prices why should they worry. If some plant is to be struck, they would much prefer that it be someone else's. So they call in the international representative and say, "Listen, Mike, you know we have always taken care of our boys, so why don't we keep going and I'll tell you now we'll do whatever the big fellow does." Free enterprise can't be preserved with that sort of courage, nor can a favorable climate of public opinion be formed by men who so little understand that patterns strangle freedom.

The skillfully directed mass labor movements reach the peak of their power at the national level, however, with the now familiar sequence of the threat of a nation-wide strike aimed at some important product or service, a widely advertised national convention or meeting of the policy group which provides the sounding board for thunderous denunciation of all of the companies in that industry, and the listing of impossible demands. Twenty to thirty seems to be about the usual number. Then comes mediation, which affords the opportunity for more press conferences, then mysterious rushings to the White House by government officials, then fact-finding by a specially appointed board, then government capitulation to another round of inflation.

Through all this welter of showmanship and pressure, collective bargaining as envisioned by those honest people who used to plead with management to meet labor half way is completely abandoned. The particular employer knows nothing at all about what is going on except what he reads in the paper. If timidly he insists upon being heard by the fact-finding board he might reluctantly be granted thirty minutes by tired men who have never before heard of his company. Gone entirely is the concept that the employer will sit down quietly around a table with his own men and in a spirit of fairness work out their differences, having in mind the special situation of that one plant in its relation to a highly competitive industry, and to the end that all may gain by making that particular company prosper. In its stead comes the pattern, the deadly sameness which destroys initiative, and which often spells disaster for a business not favored by natural circumstances, but which may nevertheless be the principal industry in the small community where it is located. The decentralization of industry now so earnestly sought by government and by thoughtful citizens cannot be fostered under the pall of national patterns. The G. I. hopefully starting his own little business in the town of his birth has stormy times ahead. A contract designed for General Motors is almost certain not to fit him. Unions call all this a drive to eliminate geographical differentials in wage scales, but in fact it is a drive to eliminate small business. With all wage rates made identical throughout the country, the big will get bigger, and the small will virtually disappear.

Consideration of this growing thirst for power by the tycoons of the modern labor movement, power that shall be coextensive with the forty-eight states geographically and that shall permeate every segment of the national economy, brings me quite logically to the subject of fact-finding boards. I suppose that every well-informed person now knows when this new tactic is being employed, but few have reflected on its implications. It could not be used if they did, for it is based by hypothesis upon public indifference. It is the way by which politicians, who hope they won't be caught at it, grant labor unions concessions which could not be obtained through collective bargaining, and which no responsible employer would agree to in a genuinely free economy. The process is quite simple. While an emergency is on, the union announces a paralyzing strike in a basic industry, and then the day before the catastrophe hits, graciously stands aside in the public interest at the request of the President to permit men from outside the industry who bear no responsibility for its welfare to determine what is best for it.

The sequence is always substantially the same before a fact-finding board. Unions never lose. Of course, they don't get all of their demands, but they always get something, and in the midst of a national emergency when sacrifice should be shared equally, an escape mechanism is set up for a favored segment of the population by which they take away from all others the something that is granted.

Now I am not one who cynically believes that a deal is made in advance. I do not say that the White House instructs the public members of fact-finding boards as to what facts they shall find or what recommendations they shall make, but my experience does lead me to believe that the White House has never appointed to such a post any man unless it is sure in advance how his mind works and what his views are likely to be.

A typical public member believes that his duty in the midst of the crisis is threefold: first, he must try to do justice between the parties; secondly, he must avert a strike; and thirdly, he must not let the head of a large union lose face. So when all the testimony is in and the last press conference has been held, he yields to expediency instead of principle and gives. After which he goes back to the campus of his university, sheds the responsibility as he resumes his academic gown, and lets others struggle to make it work. The strike, it is true, is settled, but the damage done to the economy by the cowardice of compromise may be immeasurable.

Among the three factors that influence the decisions of public members of fact-finding boards let no one underestimate the importance of the last, their unwillingness to let an important labor personality lose face. It is known in management circles as the "Phil has got to have something" principle. It operates at every level of governmental mediation and in every phase of interference in collective bargaining. I have heard it personally in I can't tell how many government conferences. We seem to be committed to a policy of balance of power among the great labor tycoons under which each in turn must make a spectacular gain for his followers. Yet, obviously, such considerations are utterly foreign to thoughtful consideration of what is best for our economy and the perpetuation of the American way of life, and totally unrelated to what is a fair wage as between a particular employer and his workmen, located in a particular community.

The prelude or build-up to the threat of a nation-wide strike from which a fact-finding board will emerge is another process which is not lovely to think about or easy to document, but which tries the souls of industrial relations staffs — I mean specifically the softening-up campaign of short, sharp strikes by small groups. They resemble the probing of enemy defenses by reconaissance patrols in war. One week it will be the shipping gang, and the next the cranemen, until a whole series of localized but repetitive incidents have occurred that harass management and create an expectancy of big things ahead in every department. The alleged grievances are always, of course, subject to orderly adjustment under the terms of the signed contract, but strikes break out instead. It is explained that the rank and file got out of hand. No one of us could prove that this is a pattern of campaign manipulated by a central authority, but it is done with consummate skill, and as the years pass and the pattern repeats itself it is hard to believe that it is purely coincidental.

The degree to which the deliberate harassing of management is contributed to or used by the communist organization in the United States is too occult for my meager sources of information. But that communism is still a force in labor strife I am very certain.

I believe that at long last most of the well-known labor leaders have turned against this sinister movement with real patriotism, but there are still many situations where their cleanup campaigns have been ineffective. There are still card-carrying communists who are officers of union locals, men who measure their own success in terms of the number of times that they are able to strike a plant in the course of a year in violation of the contract. And there is no more baffling problem in human relations than for a man who has been trained in the logical analysis of problems, and who has a lively instinct for fair dealing, to find himself face to face with such deliberate irresponsibility and planned disorder. It helps not at all at such times to have an outsider naively suggest, "Let's find out what they want." The classic picture of "sitting down around a table," the liberal employer and the well-meaning employees joining in discussion of plant problems in a spirit of mutual confidence with generous give and take on both sides becomes distorted into a nightmare of cold war in which no one wins except the enemies of our country.

Such then are some of the unlovely aspects of the exercise of power by labor unions today. They are sometimes but dimly apprehended even by those whose job it is to deal with them, and not at all by those industrialists about whose heads the labor storm has not yet broken. Yet if they are to be corrected, the whole country must be made to see them clearly, and we of the business world are the only ones who can bring that to pass.

But as we tell our story we must be scrupulously fair. Unions are here to stay, and we must accept them honestly as a permanent part of our industrial organization. Our antipathy to the things about them which we criticize must not blind us to the great values which they can contribute to our country when they with equal honesty accept the free enterprise system as something worth fighting to preserve. They can become dynamic outposts of our American democracy if they will lift their sights and accept responsibility coextensive with their present power. Within their ranks, and wearing their buttons proudly, are as fine Americans as can be found anywhere. As individuals they are almost universally hard-working good citizens. And this leads one to venture the hope that their collective conduct may soon reflect the sum total of the instinctive right-mindedness they are seen to possess when observed just as people.

Incidentally, the way to test whether a businessman

has honestly accepted the union which has been organized in his plant is to watch his policy on promotions and see whether he occasionally invites an aggressive union leader to cross over into management. If he does, he has. If he gives the next foremanship to the grievance man in the department because he is the best man, then he is being objective. This altogether wholesome practice is now going on all over the country, carrying with it a valuable cross-fertilization of ideas, and the singular thing is that this new recruit to management often has to be softened down. From being too tough on officials he sometimes switches to being too tough on workmen.

When we look at Europe we sense that in many respects the development of our labor movement has been fortunate. We have competition between different unions for members, for jurisdiction, for status and prestige. We also have a great deal of wholesome competition between employers and union leaders for the allegiance and self-interest of workers. Because of union competition employers are steadily pressed to do a better job of human relations, and the tone of this rivalry is steadily becoming more civilized. I consider this genial spirit of competition so healthy that I should greatly deplore it if one great all-embracing union ever came about in this country, and I consider it a good omen that there seems little likelihood that this will happen. If labor unions continue to keep management men on their toes, and if we in turn have the courage and intelligence to hold them up to higher standards of responsibility, the greater stability that we all seek may be closer at hand than we now believe.

CHAPTER IV **The Boss**

BUT NOTHING could be wider of the mark than to assume that reaching a satisfactory understanding with organized labor absolves the employer from all further responsibility in the field of employee relations. Whether a plant is organized or not, whether the union is independent or affiliated with a national group, whether the shop is open or closed, the boss must still remain the boss or the enterprise system has been abandoned and collectivism has set in. Our success in production rests upon decisiveness, and that is a function of individual judgment. Committees breed indecision, and divided authority stagnation. When all the conferences have been held, and all the viewpoints have been heard, there comes a time at every level of authority when one man must decide. Wars are won that way, and American production is based on that principle. But the dynamic difference between our tradition and that of production under the dictatorship that inevitably comes from collectivism is that with us the worker of today may be the boss of tomorrow if he has the stuff, and the worker who doesn't like the decisions of his boss may quit and take another job. We forget that the sacred right to quit has disappeared from the major part of the countries of the world, except ours. It is the first thing that collectivists take away.

But with us the boss who becomes arbitrary and makes a habit of wrong decisions won't be boss long. The pace is too hot, and he will be asked to stand aside if he becomes an obstruction to good teamwork. So to stay as boss at his present level of authority, and to hope that he may advance to the level above, he must not only be able to decide wisely, but he must bring it about that others will carry out his decisions with understanding and enthusiasm. He must lead and not command. And who shall tell us what leadership is, that mystic but radiant quality that some men possess, because of which others swing joyously into common action, confident that what they do is wisely conceived and eminently fair?

Surely such leadership, which is above all the characteristic of American production and a function of voluntary effort, springs from mutual understanding. The boss must know the worker and the worker must know the boss, and they must like and respect one another. Preservation of the dignity and worth of the individual demands this. No amount of money incentive will bring forth the maximum of effort without such mutual understanding. The man at the lathe in modern America must know why he is performing the task that has been assigned to him, what becomes of the formless piece of metal to which he skillfully gives useful shape, and why doing it well contributes to his own well-being through helping his company to advance in the face of competition. The boss must tell him these things, not only in letters and plant magazines but face to face, and the management man who does will be well rewarded, for this is no one-way street. The man who knows most about a lathe is the man who runs it, and if there is a better way of making that particular part he is the one most likely to come up with the new idea.

Fortunate, indeed, is the president of a smaller company located in a community of modest size. He can and usually does know every man on the payroll by his first name. He can call the employees together a group at a time, or even all at once, and tell them of the plans and hopes for the future or the problems of the present. The boss, the worker, and the town have an obvious and direct community of interest that no one can miss. But with a large company that may have plants scattered in various parts of the country the reverse is true. From a factory located in a large city twenty thousand workers may flow out of the gates each twenty-four hours to disappear into the mass of an urban population over an area fifty miles across. As the man shuts his front door when he comes home from work he shuts his company and job out of his mind, for his family have never seen the machine that he operates, and his friends hardly know the name of his company. Such inherent difficulties in the relationship make the task of industrial leadership infinitely more difficult than in the days of the beginnings of our industrial revolution, but it is the price we pay for becoming a great country, and the challenge must be met by new methods and new determination.

Organized labor is, of course, against us on this. Completely unashamed they seek a monopoly over all relationships with the worker. Though sometimes giving lip service to free enterprise in public speeches, they seek constantly to destroy the leadership upon which it rests. Steady pressure is exerted nowadays in collective bargaining by the labor professionals to enhance their own power by limiting that of management. They seek a veto power on all decisions. They want to determine who shall work at what job, or who shall be hired at all for that matter, and they wish to be the sole judges of who shall be dismissed. They want no flow of ideas from the top down in a company, and none from the bottom up except as the ideas come through them, in order that a price may be exacted. All of which denies the concept of decisiveness and leadership which gives the dynamic quality to American production. No man can successfully lead a team that he cannot choose, nor can he inspire if he is forbidden to talk. It is my firm conviction, however, that the people want it done in the traditional American way, with a boss who decides and leads, a boss whose cap any man can hope to wear; and that when they understand the problem they will vigorously reject the subtle trend toward collectivism that unions are fostering by their efforts to limit the management prerogative.

The American worker himself wants it the traditional way, and he demonstrates that by his voting in public elections. The union member wears no man's collar these days when he is alone in the voting booth. He will go out on strike all right when told to, sometimes altogether too slavishly, because he is convinced that that means money in his pocket, but he doesn't want the strike organizer to tell him how to vote. I know a coal town, for example, where the president of the local was nominated for the legislature. The men had walked out of the mine when he told them to, but they voted overwhelmingly for the other fellow when it came to choosing someone to hold public office in their behalf. Actually, I have the conviction that in these very difficult times the employees in the ordinary company are hungry to hear what the boss thinks on the problems of the day. They won't for a minute do something because he says they should, but they sense that he wouldn't be where he is if he didn't have intelligence. They sense also that his experience has given him opportunities to become informed on public questions, and before they make up their minds they would like to hear what he has to say. A wise boss tells them, tells them fairly and courageously, and lets no labor union official intimidate him.

Leadership, like everything else in life that is vital, finds its source in understanding. To be worthy of management responsibility today a man must have insight into the human heart, for unless he has an awareness of human problems, a sensitivity toward the hopes and aspirations of those whom he supervises, and a capacity for analysis of the emotional forces that motivate their conduct, the projects entrusted to him will not get ahead no matter how often wages are raised. Unhappily, this has not been our long suit so far. We have done far better with machines than with people. The all but supernatural advance that we have made in technology, and the vast physical expansion of plant that we have brought about, have not been matched by wisdom in the behavior of one man toward another, or of a gang toward the leader. To a certain degree I am afraid that this is a result of the extent to which American industry during the past generation has been dominated by the engineer and the chemist. I say this not critically. Being neither myself, I have a respect bordering upon awe for what the research and engineering geniuses have done to improve our products, but what I am talking about is management emphasis. Bankers lending money always call for a report by the engineering officer of the company, but never for one by the psychologist, although clearly, what is done with the machines after they are installed is fully as important as their design and cost. And because a man has perfected great skill in probing and testing the physical properties of metals, or glass, or liquids, which can be measured with precision instruments, it does not follow that he will be equally adept at analysis of the imponderables of the human spirit for which no caliper or test tube will be of assistance. Both gifts are seldom found in a single executive, and the wise company has men who complement each other.

All through manufacturing plants will be found bluff, hearty fellows who pride themselves on their ability to "handle men." Actually they do and can handle men constituted as they are, usually by the direct and simple method of knocking two heads together. But in every walk of life there are people whose "handling" requires subtlety, who can be led but not driven, for whom a kind and sympathetic word will do more than all the invective yet invented. Actually, the use of praise when due, and fair criticism when that is due, are the two most powerful attributes of wise leadership, particularly in dealing with the imaginative and creative personalities so much neded in industry, yet all too few men employ them. A job well done is apt to be taken for granted: that is what the fellow is hired for. And a job badly done can block a man's further usefulness if the bawling out he gets fails to discriminate between what was actually his fault and what was not. Our integrity is at stake in these matters, for those supervised are constantly measuring us for signs of our interest in them as persons, and unless they believe in us, they will not follow us.

Progressive management today, finding itself compelled to struggle with human problems as never before, and feeling at times altogether baffled by them, has a new tool at hand in the services of the industrial psychological consultant. This new profession is spreading rapidly across the country, and those who scoffed have stayed to pray. As the social sciences have come to maturity in the universities, students have been graduated into industry who have an awareness of the problems of human behavior, and now the Ph.D. in psychology is prepared to set up a program of research into friction between people on a par with that of the Ph.D. in metallurgy into friction between metals. Both are needed to achieve improved production.

The first thing of course that the consultant will undertake will be to help the executive to understand himself. The boss becomes a better man when he looks at himself through the eyes of another. He sees, for example, that his hot flashes of anger do not in fact bring beneficial results, that his receptivity to ideas offered to him by others is low, that animosity is not necessarily lurking behind criticism, that habitual attitudes of which he was unaware stand in the way of his getting full loyalty from his subordinates. Only when he can be objective in a critical analysis of himself is he prepared to study the motivations of others.

As his horizons begin to widen in this challenging field he attacks the familiar personnel difficulties with new zest and new confidence. He senses that there is a lot to be done other than just knocking two heads together, and that much human endeavor can be salvaged that has been going to waste all through the organization. In fact, this may be as good a way to lower costs as to put in new machines. And of such stuff is leadership made.

The range of human problems that exist in industry is as broad as human nature itself, and often extraordinarily disconcerting. Take, for example, the case of the man who refuses a promotion. I suspect that a great many people think of a steel company as a vast collection of men who work under difficult and dangerous surroundings, and who are ground down by economic circumstance, forever doomed to frustration though burning with ambition and endowed with great natural gifts. Nothing could be further from the fact. So far as safety is concerned, the man working underground in an iron mine is safer than his wife who will probably cut her hand in the kitchen or slip in the bathtub, and as for opportunity, leadership is still the scarcest commodity in the world. Management is constantly on the prowl for it, and greatly disconcerted when the man to whom promotion is offered spends a few sleepless nights worrying over it, finally faces up to his own limitations, turns it down, and walks out of the boss' office a happy man.

The boss has planned that move for a long time, and feels badly let down, but maybe the man was right. Possibly his insight into his own limitations was a more reliable guide than that of his superior officer. And possibly he has values in his life that are not glimpsed in the limited outlook of his boss. Could be that the job isn't the end-all of life, as it seems to be to the boss. Perhaps it is only a means to permit him to pursue the real passion of his life, which might be fancy skating, or painting, or caring for an invalid wife whom he loves, or preaching the faith of his forefathers.

A corollary is that of the man who has been promoted and doesn't measure up. Manfully he tries to throw himself into a task for which his inner self tells him he is not fitted, and as his doubts increase those who have pinned their hopes on him begin to have their doubts, too. Eventually all concerned sense that they have locked themselves into an intolerable situation. At last the boss screws up his courage to tell the man that it won't do, and that he will have to go back to the old job, sometimes to be met with tears of gratitude. An important bit of human salvage has been achieved, and the organization functions more smoothly than before.

And then of course there is the whole gamut of forces that exist in a man's life off the job that reduce his effectiveness while in the plant, about which something can be done if the proper relationship exists: insight on the part of the superior and confidence on the part of the man. If a crane operator thinks his wife has been unfaithful to him, the chances are that he will cause an accident, and no amount of automatic devices or safety rules will prevent it. If the son of a foreman is caught red-handed by the police in an act of burglary, the foreman's gang will not meet its normal quota of production the next day. A man's own health may become such an obsession with him that his effectiveness is cut in half when all that is needed is a proper diagnosis to prove to him that he has no serious problem at all. Over and over again, when the light of psychological research is turned on the dark and unexplored recesses of industrial organization, new situations are brought to light that bear on production where improvement can be obtained, either at once or over the long pull, but which have gone undiscovered for lack of an awareness of and interest in human problems on the part of management. If the battle of free enterprise is to be won, these new skills must be mastered, for the men we would lead we must first understand.

CHAPTER V The Businessman and
the Community

BUT SKILLED LEADERSHIP within the industrial organization is not enough. It will increase production, and
that the free world needs desperately, but of itself it
will not solve the social problems that threaten to
destroy the very system of production upon which
our national welfare depends. Our blind spot as businessmen is our failure to sense compelling personal responsibility for the perpetuation of that system, our
naive belief that we have done our part when we break
the production records, and that we may leave to
others the defense of free enterprise. There are no
others. Christianity was not carried to the heathen by
atheists, nor communism to the satellites by capitalists.
We and we alone must be the ones to hold aloft the
symbol of our faith that the driving power and infinite
ingenuity of private initiative make more people happy
than planning by the cloistered few.

But to win converts we must have an audience, and right now our public isn't listening. Our words fall on deaf ears, not because they lack truth, but rather because of who we are that speak them. Specifically, the rather grim fact is that the American businessman is no longer the natural leader in his community. His father and his grandfather were. They cut the forest, broke the prairie to the plow, and built crude forges to make iron, but they also hewed with their own hands the timbers for the village church, and set aside section 16 in every township for the school. The miracle of production had not yet wrought its hypnosis on the minds of men to whom God gave the gift of leadership, and they knew that the welfare of all was the responsibility of each. We have far outstripped them in tons per man, but are unworthy sons in terms of civic consciousness.

I think, for example, of a noble man whose simple but glorious life I took for granted as a boy in the village where I was born. He was literally the village blacksmith. I still recall the hiss of the hot iron as he plunged it into his tub of water, and see in my mind the flash of his knife as he trimmed the hoof held by hand and knee against his leather apron. All the tough farm jobs were brought to him because he was the best blacksmith anywhere in our part of the country. But it was the life he lived when he left the shop that made him the leader in our community. He was the superintendent of our Sunday School and taught my sister and me the ten commandments; he was the president of our Board of Education and signed my diploma when I graduated from high school; and when his fame had spread, as it was bound to do, he was elected to the State Legislature as the representative from our district. How vast and immediate would be the enhancement of our prestige if every industrial leader who breaks a production record could also be pointed to as the man who broke a record in character forming, better schools, and better politics.

The means by which we do this are at hand, even in the great metropolitan areas. We are a nation of voluntary organizations, and it may be that when the history of our times is written this characteristic will stand out as our most revolutionary contribution to the advancement of human welfare by democratic processes. It is the precise antithesis to central planning, for it preserves the wisdom of the many while harnessing the power of aroused individual responsibility. In the twenties it was fashionable to laugh at all this, to ridicule Babbitt, but in the sober fifties we are still trying to recapture the values lost in the complacency and sophistication of those years. Certainly it is this characteristic which today distinguishes Europe from the United States in the general attack upon social problems. They have only the most rudimentary and feeble counterparts for our voluntary associations of citizens who share a common interest and are determined to strive unselfishly and tirelessly to achieve a common end. Personally, I am glad that Babbitt was an American. Let them have socialism, let them have the dead hand of collectivism where the government knows all and does all, while the citizen waits for someone else to do it, but give me the hustle and earnestness of the Rotary, the League of Women Voters, the Community Chest, the Red Cross, and all that infinite variety of committee action that is indigenous to America. It is sometimes ludicrous, and often wasteful, but it is democracy at work. Only I wish that we might see more such committees headed by a businessman, instead of by his public relations officer, or a professional uplifter.

Take the Community Chest, for example, or as we call it in Chicago, the Community Fund. Can any accomplishment of our technology surpass in significance this unique American invention for clearing away the human wreckage which our mass production has brought in its train? When industry faces up to its obligations to the social agencies represented by its Community Chest, it recognizes that social problems are here to stay, that hereafter there will be no social vacuums, and that either we will meet the needs of our communities in forthright fashion by voluntary effort, or government will step in, thus marching us another long step down the road toward socialism and the ultimate extinguishment of free enterprise. We cannot have it both ways: we cannot pursue our own interests and ignore those of others, for if we turn our back on the community, it will shortly turn its back on us.

All of this is clearly perceived by any large company which moves into a remote area to build a new plant. Workmen must be attracted, and the personnel manager is keenly sensitive to the fact that no proud American who has the required skills will move his family out into the sticks where they must live under sub-normal conditions, just for money. So the company lays out an attractive town site, builds modern homes, and sets about seeing that there are schools and hospitals and churches, and all the things that make for good living. But when the same social needs are concealed beneath the drab blankets of confusion and the

impersonal vastness of a great city, not so many corporate executives have the imagination and character
to sense a direct necessity for effort on their part with
respect to the hidden distress. Let a frail and elderly
lady fall to the sidewalk on a busy street and ten men
in that block will rush to her aid. If she is obviously in
want there is sure to be one who will take her home in
a cab, and as he leaves he will press a ten dollar bill in
her hand, his heart warm for the rest of the day because of what he has done. But give him a card from
the Community Fund representing a call of solicitation
he should make on a neighboring firm, that all frail
women in that great city who are in want may have a
ten dollar bill pressed into their hands by a trained
social worker, and he may put it off for a week, or perhaps not do it at all.

Quite unwittingly, in fact in hot anger, I once
created a legend. While campaigning for the Community Fund, I went to speak at the Produce Exchange in Chicago. I was to spring into action when
the gong sounded for the close of trading and try to
catch the attention of the traders while they were still
grouped in the pit. In front of me stood a very fat man.
As the gong struck I was eager to start, but the zealous
chairman droned on with a verbose introduction. The

fat man grew suspicious of what was coming, and as the words Community Fund were pronounced he started for the door. I had been working pretty hard in the campaign, and in a flash I was incandescent with anger. Without taking thought I cried out in a loud voice, "Look at that fat man going out the door." The man froze in his tracks, and a startled hush came over the crowd, but I was too mad to stop, so I went on, saying, "That fat man thinks he is walking out on the Community Fund, but he isn't. He is walking out on an old lady dying of cancer in an attic, and a little baby who was born the day after her father was killed in a saloon can't have her eyes saved from blindness because that fat man doesn't care." It was brutal, it happened just that way, and people tell me that my fat man story is still being told in Community Chest campaigns around the country.

One of the important by-products of personal participation in a community fund campaign, or any other form of community activity, is the broadening of friendships and the widening of horizons that it brings. As businessmen we tend to become inbred. We live so intensely with our own problems that we come to think of them as the most important ones in the world. It comes as a shock to us to find that others do not so regard them. We work together, eat together, and play together until our opinions reflect the lowest common denominator of the thinking of our own particular group. But as we are suddenly thrust into intimate association with men from other forms of business activity, and particularly with those who come from fields totally unrelated to business, all in pursuit of a public cause, we experience a most salutary corrective on the extremes of our opinions. We gain a new perspective, a new humility, and a suspicion that perhaps we are not quite as right as we thought. This is especially true as between management and labor. When a company official and a union business agent work side by side for a few weeks to raise money for an orphanage they are apt to discover to their mutual surprise that the other fellow is after all pretty much of a regular guy. And that leads to the wholesome inner thought that maybe the fellow on the opposite side of the table in collective bargaining is also a regular guy.

But for this the personal activity of the executive is required. Community responsibility cannot be delegated. You cannot hire someone to be a good neighbor for you. It is a job for every man himself at every echelon of authority if the public is to be persuaded that we think free enterprise really makes their lives better. They want to hear from you, not your agent. The way to understand why the foreign-born worker brings his alien ideology into the plant is for the boss himself to try to teach him English and Americanism in a settlement house, and the best approach to the demand for socialized medicine is for the businessman himself to serve on the board of a hospital and spend some time in the out-patient department. When we tell ourselves that we are too busy and too important to the enterprise to do these things personally, and when we ask someone on the staff to do them for us, that man knows we have ducked. He will then duck, too, doing just as little as he can without getting caught. And once a company gets the reputation of ducking its community responsibilities, no one will listen to its officers when they pound the table and say that free enterprise must be saved. Actions still speak louder than words.

Personal participation means also, of course, generous giving to community causes. Most businessmen think that they give generously to charity, but actually there is disparity as between men of equal earnings that is quite shocking when you see the figures. Making all due allowance for private circumstances which no outsider should try to assess, the fact remains that some businessmen are very generous and others very selfish. And some are merely careless, in that after several promotions and substantial increases in compensation they still give on the scale they established as young men.

Then what about corporate giving, the direct money contributions from business as such to the voluntary agencies that exist about us for advancement of the welfare of the society which bestows on us the privilege of production for private profit? I hold the deep conviction, of course, that the meeting of the social needs of the community is a proper charge to the cost of production. It is not charity, but the acceptance of responsibility. I note, for example, that Russia has no community fund but no private business either. Time was when corporation lawyers wrote profound legal opinions to the effect that a gift to a hospital, or a library, or a college was *ultra vires*, beyond the powers of the board of directors as expressed in the charter, but a most wholesome up-surge of public opinion with regard to this important subject is fast breaking down that barrier. How can it be *ultra vires* for a corporation to strive to preserve the form of society which alone makes possible the continuation of the business?

It used to be said that it was not for the board to decide how the stockholders should dispose of their money, but what little sense that made. It might just as well be said that the board ought not to repair broken machinery because it represented the stockholders' money.

Take the case of a company that operates a plant in Chicago. More than likely it has stockholders in each of the forty-eight states. Is it reasonable to suppose that a stockholder owning twenty shares who lives in Rhode Island will be aware of the serious deficit at a colored hospital on Chicago's south side, and so moved by the need, that he will write to inquire if a campaign is on and send in a contribution? Yet if that hospital is just around the corner from the plant and the company ignores its manifest and urgent need, the neighborhood will deteriorate, good workmen will move away, production will fall, and dividends will have to be curtailed. It is just that simple when good management faces up realistically to the fact that the meeting of social need is as much a cost of production as plant maintenance.

Mention of a colored hospital (and why should there be colored hospitals as such?) leads naturally to the next question on which the businessman who hopes to have prestige in the community must assert leadership, and that is the integration of minority groups into the working forces. Straight thinking and a cool head are required here, but I hold the view that we have magnified the problem into something that appears to be far more formidable than it really is. With the matter reduced to its simplest terms, it would seem to be clear that merit should be the sole test for employment and for promotion. As between two candidates, the best man should always get the job if low cost production is our goal. Ability is not a function of color. When the steel industry imports a train load of Mexicans to perform the manual tasks around its open hearth furnaces, it must receive them into equal partnership with all other workmen, and accept the responsibility of guiding them toward citizenship. They must not be regarded as disposable items. Nor must we permit ourselves to be diverted from our obvious duty by the emotion and hysteria with which this subject has often been surrounded. The way to integrate is to integrate, and it is surprising how easily it can be done when we really try.

I am not sure that legislation has helped in those states where it has been attempted. Such laws are directed at the employer, and enforcement is attempted through hiring policy. There may be such, but I do not recall having heard of a law making it a misdemeanor for a white man to refuse to work alongside a Negro, or the converse, yet the usual deterrent to management is the belief that a brittle attitude on this subject exists among his employees which he himself is unable to control no matter how advanced his views. On the other hand, in support of laws, I would have to admit, to our shame, that as businessmen we sometimes do things where there is a law which all along we have known was right but have never put into practice.

As a matter of fact, attitudes are as important for a company in the field of community relations as actions, and there is another whole category of subjects where what should have been done as a matter of conscience has been forced upon us by law. I mean pollution of air and water, noise, traffic congestion, and all the other controllable nuisances which we have imposed upon our long-suffering neighbors. I am as impatient as the next man about captious criticism, for heavy production cannot be carried on in a vacuum and a certain amount of inconvenience must be tolerated if we are to get ahead with the job; but to go on doing something we know we can stop just because we can get away with it is not playing fair with the public. When they hit back, it is no wonder that they hit hard. Integrity is the basis of confidence, and how can we expect the public to care what our economic views are so long as we pump raw sewage or smelly liquids into the lake or river from which they draw their drinking water? And the housewife who can't hang out her wash without running the risk that it will be blackened with dust from our chimneys is not apt to be particularly impressed with our opinions on inflation.

Noise is another sore spot, and one to which we have applied very little of our vaunted technological genius. We sound-proof our own offices to soften the click of our secretary's electric typewriter, but who is to sound-proof the home of the young mother down the street from our plant whose baby wakes whenever our whistle blows, and who cares far more about that curly head than about who is spending our taxes? And, for that matter, while we are giving a little consideration to the ears of our neighbors, we might think a little about their eyes. The design of an American plant is dictated by how it will work, not how it will look, yet so often we could plan for both without added cost if we could establish the right habit of mind.

When I visited the new steel plant at Margam, Wales, I was struck by the fact that it looked like none I had ever seen before. When I asked about it I found this unique explanation. After the engineers had laid out the plant to functional perfection as they saw it, the management called in an architect who had never before done industrial work of that sort in order that he might give the structures line and dignity. No additional cost was involved, but the result was something new and pleasing, of which all concerned are very proud.

Traffic congestion is another source of friction between industry and the community. The American worker is determined to come to work in an automobile, and quite understandably he wants to leave it in a safe place when he goes on the job. The result is acres upon acres of shiny new cars that must be disposed of while the wheels of industry turn. My European friends tell me that on coming here for the first time they find this to be the most staggering index of our power and of our prosperity, and they smile a little as we struggle with parking, for over there it would be bicycles, and a bicycle can be hung on a rack. Actually, this phenomenon has two aspects of social significance. First is the pride of ownership, which every one of us has in some degree and which is in itself an incentive toward effective effort. When a new car shows up on the lot the rest of the boys want one too and will work hard to get it. And even if there is a bus they will bring the car to show it off, and to satisfy their urge for complete independence. And the other is the amazing mobility that the private car gives the labor force of an area, which has no counterpart anywhere in the world. But what a headache it gives management. It is all very well for a new plant built on vacant prairies to lay out parking space almost as large as that required for the productive processes, but for older plants which are locked in by densely built-up areas, it is almost impossible of solution. The worker knows that, and so does the small businessman whose store is blocked all day with employee cars, and all that they ask is evidence that we care and are trying. Consideration for others is the crux of it. Even if there isn't a single vacant lot to be had, we can study public transportation intelligently and try to improve train and bus service.

And what about housing? Here is a subject that would try men's souls if there ever was one, and most of us have been walking out on it for a long, long time, particularly in the large cities. We jump in our cars at the end of the day and drive to our suburb, proud to tell the little woman of how the plant broke its shipping record that day, unmindful of the gradual deterioration that is taking place in living conditions in the area around the plant from which our normal labor supply should come. Eventually, and imperceptibly, a process of strangulation begins. The personnel manager reports an increasing number of work force requisitions unfilled, and comments that skilled and responsible men are especially hard to get, but still we may be blind to cause and effect. Actually, if the plant is an older one, the city has grown away from it. What used to be a residential section is now heavily industrialized so that the houses which remain are in unpleasant surroundings, and subjected to the industrial noise, dirt, and danger which do not make for good living. The new plants of the area are being built out on the edge of the city where the ambitious young man just starting his family can have fresh air and good schools and churches for his children. He forsakes the older industrial area and signs on with the new, and the old tends to get only those workers who are rejected by the new.

This is a serious problem for many of the older companies today, and they are driven by sheer self-interest to make up for their years of deficit in community cooperation. But what to do about housing is most baffling. One thing is certain: it is not wise for the employer suddenly to appropriate a large sum of capital and build houses for rental. There are enough sources of friction in the relationship of employer and employee already without adding that of landlord and tenant. And if we wish to reverse the trend toward looking to others for security in life, we should begin by encouraging the worker to own his own home. Pride in ownership is an essential part of pride in America and pride in the way of life we are seeking to preserve, and we must have no part in breaking that down.

There are many things we can do, however, to stimulate the grass roots desire for neighborhood improvement which can always be found in every community. For example, we can employ consultants to lay out a suggested master plan for the area to the end that earlier mistakes will not be repeated. We can make capital available by way of loan for the building of homes, although that is seldom necessary nowadays when so many lending agencies are seeking sound investments. It is know-how that is needed, and above all the radiant quality of leadership. The good citizen who sees his neighborhood going to pieces around him feels a crushing sense of personal futility. He doesn't see that there is anything he can do about it all by himself. But he is electrified when suddenly he finds that the boss is on his team, and will work his heart out to bring about better things as soon as he thinks there is a chance for success. Management interest is the assurance he needs.

And so one could go on touching on other phases of the relationship between the businessman and his community, but it seems abundantly clear that we cannot influence public opinion by production alone. The old adage of handsome is as handsome does is still true. People around us will respect us if we show consideration for their welfare and share their problems, and will most certainly ignore us if we do not.

CHAPTER VI The Businessman and
the Government

ONE PROBLEM that as businessmen we have been a little
loath to share is that of government. At every echelon,
from the ward and precinct in which we live up
through Congress and the foreign service, we have
been inclined to leave the job of government to others,
though reserving to the full our right to criticize, and
to assume that somewhere there is a great leisure group
of able men who can and will do these things for the
love of them. We have raised ridicule of office holders
to a fine art, and have demanded in no uncertain terms
that there be more government for the people, but
have laid less emphasis on the fact that government is
also supposed to be by the people, and that we are
those people.

I have not been without some small reputation myself in the matter of denunciation of public officials,
and I retract no single word. For a generation business

has tried to live and to make progress under a barrage of abuse and misrepresentation from those who have been elected to high office — so violent and so continuous that historians may wonder how free enterprise survived at all. Perhaps there could be no stronger proof of its essential vitality than the fact that we still have it. The big guns of government have been trained against us at all times, using our money to supply the ammunition, and attack has followed attack in successive waves — at all times, that is, except when government has needed us badly.

The people have been told, for example, that big business is bad, and particularly that it stifles small business, in spite of the fact that never in our history have so many new and successful small enterprises been begun as in the past ten years. But whenever a big job has needed doing, government has invariably turned to big business with the desperation of urgent need, and been grateful that great resources and vast facilities created by private industry could be made available immediately. Russia has had to build hers the hard way: ours were ready. You can't build a battleship in a neighborhood machine shop, or ask a popcorn vender to roll a hundred thousand tons of ship plates a month. Likewise, when national defense has brought into being a job so exacting in its requirements of knowledge and background, and so breathtaking in its responsibility that not even the hardiest of politicians has dared tackle it, government has turned to business for the leadership. Such fitness is acquired only by a lifetime of experience with comparable problems, and cannot be improvised by a country school teacher or even a labor leader, no matter how able or how devoted to the public service. But these are exceptional cases, and direct participation by businessmen in public administration is at a low ebb. Whether it is more because government doesn't ask us until they are in desperate straits or because we look out the window and ignore the call to duty I am not clear, but certain it is that the result is unwholesome for both business and the public, and that something should be done about it. One of our nation's greatest reserves of manpower in terms of creative leadership is not being fully employed for the common good.

We need a new tradition of public service, a new habit of mind by which businessmen actively seek participation in public affairs at every level. Like charity, this should begin at home. Each one of us lives somewhere, and whether that be a city apartment, a suburban house, or a farm in the country we receive constantly the benefit of public services for which some elected official must in a democracy assume the responsibility. Why should someone else invariably do those things for us? Is our production job more important than maintaining the very fabric of democracy that permits it to exist? Is it fair to bewail the venality of weak men who corrupt offices of public trust which we abandon to them by our own default? Actually, of course, we should begin as young men, doing such essential jobs as precinct worker and watcher at the polls, and then keeping our part-time public service in parallel with our business advancement by serving as members of school and park boards or city councils, until we serve terms in our state legislature or Congress, or take occasional appointments in Washington. And every business institution that believes in the preservation of free enterprise should make this possible, and encourage us to do so. We will be better men when we return, and the business will have a stronger team in that substitutes will be trained and tested in our absence. Nor am I concerned at what this will cost in money, since the unbelievable cost of letting others do these jobs for us has already been fully demonstrated.

The federal government is continuously in urgent

need of competent staff. We can no longer usefully debate whether the United States should have a compelling and demanding position of leadership in the free world: we have it, and there will be no drawing back in this generation. The proliferation of government agencies is beyond numbering, and whether we like them or whether we don't, there they are. It is our money that is being spent. There is no reservoir of talent upon which to draw to staff these agencies because the United States has had no tradition of public service as a career, and many a harassed official is carrying on with a mediocre staff because he can get no better. He has to make do with what he has, and gets little help from us even in the wise spending of the money which our elected representatives have voted to him.

Lend-lease of talent is the answer. I hold the earnest belief that it is a proper function for business to supply staff to government on a term basis, and that this is a proper charge against our cost of production. If the job is being badly done, and our management brains and skill can help to do it better, everyone gains. Take our junior executives, for example. Over the long pull, wouldn't it be a fine thing if every young man with a future, and we all know who some of them are in our companies, should go to Washington for two years and take a government job, either here or abroad? They serve in war, why not in peace, only here they would have our full financial backing. If they are half as good as we think they are they might collectively save us more money in two years of service with the government than they possibly could by staying at their desks in our plants and offices. Government would steadily receive a new transfusion of blood and at the same time meet its huge staff deficit, to say nothing of the general increase in mutual understanding that would be brought about. Career people would develop new respect for the standards of ability and integrity that prevail in business, while the young men would come back broadened by the impact of unusual responsibilities, and perhaps a little more humble than we are with respect to understanding the difficulties of public administration. But of course we can do none of this until our laws are changed to permit business to reimburse fully the added expense of living away from home for those who are willing to make the great personal sacrifice required. I have never personally known or seen documented a case where a businessman whether young or old has used such a position to help unfairly either himself or his company, and it is the maddest sort of folly to deny good citizens, both corporate and individual, this avenue for serving our country by not letting their companies hold their incomes level.

Consider, for example, the altogether extraordinary situation in which we find ourselves as a nation with respect to military spending. Surely at no other time in the history of the world have so few had so much to spend. The sums of money appropriated for defense by Congress in recent years and still unspent stagger the imagination. Experts disagree as to precisely what the colossal total is, and the margin of difference between the estimates is greater than the entire national debt as of the time when I first remember learning that there was a national debt. I have been deeply conscious of the responsibility involved in the spending since 1945 of the sums of money appropriated for plant expansion by the board of directors of the company for which I work, which are tremendous by earlier standards, yet all of that capital would hardly make a first-class typographical error in the current budgets of the army, navy, and air forces. In fact, all of the sums spent by all of the major steel companies during the same period for the greatest increase in production capacity the world has ever known would scarcely make a down payment on what the generals and admirals are undertaking.

I know generals. I served on the staff of one in the first war, and have the most profound respect for their intelligence and devotion to duty. As a nation we have been fortunate in the outstanding quality of the generals and admirals who have risen to the posts of top responsibility in this generation, but no man can know everything or have time enough in his life to acquire every type of experience. Is it reasonable to believe, therefore, that these men in addition to their proven judgment and experience in professional matters possess as a group greater capacity as administrators by several times over than all of the officers of all of the steel companies, who have made the prudent spending of other people's money their life-time profession? Congress, of course, has no further control over the sums already appropriated. For the most part our elected representatives who are charged with responsibility for the expenditure of tax monies have abdicated, and glad they were, I suspect, to do so, for the word defense is now so sacrosanct that one who questions this vast program is apt to be suspected of disloyalty. Should not the business organizations, therefore, whose broad backs must bear the principal burden of this enormous cost seek a chance to review the program, and advise with respect to the manner of the spending? We know, as every good citizen does, that the danger is tragically real and that doubt must always be resolved in favor of security and still more security for America, but is it unreasonable to ask that men who have shown outstanding ability in the wise expenditure of large sums of money be given a place at the council table in this time of grave emergency? Surely it must be clear that we have not made the world safe if by our efforts we destroy the American economy and our free enterprise system.

But if leaders of industry have been reluctant to accept positions in government or to lend their staff when asked to do so, or have failed to assert themselves with respect to the spending of public funds when not asked, their counterparts in big labor have displayed no such diffidence. Persistently and quietly they have caused their staffs to infiltrate into every federal agency. The "clear it with Sidney" principle has been carried down to the lowest echelons of government by the politicians. Those in the know call it the American Politburo. Overseas, for example, you will find a labor adviser not only in every principal embassy and legation, but in each of the country missions established for the distribution of economic aid.

Some of these men have made outstanding contributions, and have demonstrated that they are Americans first and union men secondly. I think of one whose personal background and philosophy are as diverse from mine as could possibly be, for whom I have great respect and affection. He was in his day not only an active socialist, but a nose-punching union organizer who led bloody strikes, yet I would back him now to the limit for any job to which he might be nominated. He has great integrity and marked administrative ability, and serves the United States admirably. In fact, he is a better man in my opinion than many businessmen who have tried to advise him. But I am bound to say that I believe such instances to be exceptional. Organized labor seems to arrogate to itself the right to be set above the general level of our citizenship, and expects to exercise a special veto power over policies formed and decisions taken by the representatives of all of the people. That must not be. It would be equally wrong if attempted by the National Association of Manufacturers, or the United States Chamber of Commerce. We serve our country as Americans and not as agents of special interests, and when we put on the cap of authority we must remove all private insignia.

One further and unrelated word needs to be said before leaving the subject of the businessman vis-à-vis government, and that is simply this: we deny our heritage and jeopardize free enterprise when we ask special consideration for our own industry or our own company. If we seek to keep government out of business we must not ourselves invite it in. Take all sorts of subsidy, for example. The crudest form of this is merely to ask Uncle Sam to provide the capital which we have not been able to raise from private sources, to let him build the plants which we will operate for private gain. I am not, of course, referring to a war-time facility that has no peace-time counterpart, which is managed for a fee, but rather to the easy touch for money made with the tongue in the cheek. Of all ways to bring on the nationalization of industry that would seem to be the most effective, for what the people pay for they will ultimately run. Free enterprise means private capital, and the man who dares not risk is unworthy to share in the rewards.

Indirect subsidy is far more difficult to detect, but it can be found in all varieties of preferential rates and special means of protection. Those who seek it have many pious disguises, and those who give it expect many improper compensations. Each time it happens a fraud is perpetrated on the public, the integrity of our economy is weakened, and the broad path to socialism made smoother.

Having urged the businessman to participate in government, what shall I say of his participation in partisan politics? Here the what not to do is easy to state. Under no circumstances may he attempt, either directly or indirectly, to use economic power to influence the voting of those whom he supervises. That day is happily gone forever, and he must hew to the line scrupulously even though he sees frantic efforts on the labor side to do the opposite. But this does not mean that he must remain colorless or neutral in the midst of a political campaign. Like every other citizen he should stand up and be counted, whether it be for a principle in which he believes or a candidate whom he admires. He must not lean over backward until he appears ridiculous, for the price of leadership is that one must always stand for something. This means that it is a perfectly normal phenomenon for two executive officers of the same company to be publicly known as belonging to opposite political parties, and to campaign for opposite principles or different candidates. Most of us shrink from partisan politics as something a little unclean, but the reason the professionals have such an easy time of it is that the amateurs stay off the course. The two-party system, one in power and one in opposition, both vigorous and healthy, is the best device yet found for carrying on the vast business of this great republic, and to the extent that it falters we must share our part of the blame. If businessmen genuinely seek a new place of leadership in our country we must enter readily into every level of activity in which the public interest is involved. But in so doing we must drop our negative habit of mind. We cannot exercise leadership in our community or the nation just by being against things; we must know what things we think ought to be done and be for them fearlessly.

CHAPTER VII Self-Interest

LET US SUPPOSE now that the problem of the reestablishment of community leadership by the businessman has been solved, and that people of all sorts, both those with whom we work and those who have never heard of our companies and wouldn't be excited about them if they did, come to believe that what we say might be worth listening to and might reach into their own sphere of self-interest — what is it that we want to tell them? Suppose the invisible moderator of public opinion suddenly turns to us and says, "You are on the air, and all America is listening." Can we handle that broadcast, or will we freeze at the mike?

No one of us alone can but all of us together can if each of us knows his script. But it must be his own. No one can write it for him. Just as the strength of our production lies in the infinite variety of our skills, the ever changing kaleidoscope of ingenuity applied in techniques, so our effective force in the realm of public opinion will depend upon the intense individuality of our thinking, both as to ideas and as to scale of values. It is the distilled wisdom of the many that is America's greatest natural resource. There is no single and readily discernible right answer to any of our great social and economic questions, but as the evidence piles up, as man after man stands up to be counted by declaring what he himself believes to be true, the probable outline of the best course to follow begins to appear on the radar of our national consciousness. No dictatorship which bases policy on the wisdom of the few can possibly outmatch such a source of strength.

No single industrialist can, of course, have personal knowledge or experience in all of the controversial areas of debate today, both domestic and foreign, although as he advances in understanding he will come to see that there are few that do not affect the welfare of his particular company in the long run. But each can follow his own bent, and as each becomes intelligently articulate as to the subject which for him gives the most challenge, the normal play of natural forces created by differences in background, education, and personality will inevitably bring it about that the influence of businessmen will be brought to bear on all subjects. Then gradually the interrelationship of problems that seem to be diverse will emerge, and basic ideas will appear to which all of us can give common devotion.

The place to start, of course, is with the profit and loss system of production under private management, and the first people with whom to seek complete mutuality of understanding are our employees. What are the common errors or lapses of their economic thinking from our viewpoint? If we do not know, we have at hand the modern tool of the private opinion poll, which has already rocked many a management group out of its vulnerable complacency. But even before that report comes in we have good reason to suspect that many ideas which we regard as so obvious and clear as not to require discussion, are either distorted or denied by those who have not yet had the opportunity to try to run a business.

The first is the part that profit plays. In the lexicon of organized labor, the word profit is often used as a term of opprobrium, with the insidious suggestion being planted in the union member's mind that it is something which corporations achieve dishonorably. Extortionate is the customary adjective. And the amount of profit if expressed in dollars is never stated in relation to the dollars of capital invested in the plant and machinery of the company, so that a judgment can be formed as to whether, all things considered, one is reasonable in relation to the other. Profit as the workhorse that makes the whole thing go is never portrayed, the sole authorized symbol being the paunchy man with the big cigar being helped out of his limousine by his chauffeur. I remember once, for example, when as part of an organizing drive the union said of our company, "Their profits are plenty adequate." It is good form in these days when communism is no longer a safe bedfellow politically, for a labor leader in a public speech to declare his belief in free enterprise. However, you will seldom find him telling his followers that the earning of profits is essential to the preservation of the system, and that the larger the profit in a particular company, the greater the security and hope of increased wages for the worker.

Actually, profit is the sole source of capital for plant expansion and the creation of new jobs: directly through that portion of earnings which are retained in the business, and indirectly through creating the incentive by which the thrifty who have saved money are persuaded to invest new capital in that business. A move to limit business profits is a move to limit the industrial expansion of America, a move to limit jobs, and a move to limit our standard of living. If it were desirable to limit profits, surely it would be more desirable to prohibit them, and that would bring us at one stroke to full blown totalitarianism. The state alone would provide the capital and run every business. There would then be no necessity to contain Russia, for we could embrace her. We would have accepted her way of life.

What I now say will be somewhat controversial and displeasing to many, but if one is to have a clear personal business philosophy, and contribute vigorously to the development of public opinion through discussion, he must say what he thinks. I happen to believe that confusion has been introduced into our efforts to explain the relationship of profits to the well-being of our economy by the use of the phrase profit-sharing, and the suggestion that it describes a cure-all for disputes between management and labor. If the word profit is employed to designate that portion of the selling price which is set aside as compensation for the providing of capital through self-denial by the saver, and if the incentive thus provided is what induces saving and risk-taking, then a division of that compensation through so-called sharing with those who have neither saved nor risked will necessarily reduce the incentive to those who should be persuaded to do so and thus retard the flow of capital required for an expanding economy. In other words, I consider the phrase profit-sharing to be an inaccurate use of words.

What is a fair wage, and what is an effective reward for the risking of savings are entirely separate things to be determined by the play of economic and social forces in our society. No profit, for example, is extortionate if achieved by intelligence and energy in the face of vigorous competition. If a large profit can be won easily under those conditions others will rush in to share it and prices will fall through competition, while if it is small new savings will be withheld and that industry will deteriorate.

What the proponents of profit-sharing really mean, in my opinion, is a method for the payment of wages by which a man senses a direct response between his effort and his pay. That is an altogether sound principle, and one which is employed everywhere throughout production, although it is usually opposed by the very labor unions who advocate profit-sharing. It is present, for example, in every form of piece work, and there reflects the American tradition which is concerned with the worth of the particular citizen. There is no individual justice, nor is there fairness to the community as a whole in paying the same wage to all regardless of effort. The man who contributes more to society must be paid more or we go straight to socialism. Many occupations do not lend themselves to piece work pay, however, and there the group production bonus has become commonplace. All through the steel industry, for example, it has always been customary to establish a bogie for the tonnage to be turned out by an appropriate team, and then to pay a bonus for excess tons produced to be distributed rateably among the members of the group. It is sometimes suggested that this be attempted for a company as a whole, but with such large units the difficulties of administration become almost insurmountable, and the dilution such that no incentive remains. It becomes hard for the man to believe that his effort makes any difference, and it is much more satisfactory from every point of view to keep it within such natural limits that the direct relation between effort and compensation remains clear.

For the employee who wishes to enter into profit-sharing in its true sense the way is open. All he has to do is to share the risk-taking by investing his savings in his company's stock. And how many problems would advance toward solution if this altogether wholesome practice could become widespread. This is so obvious that one wonders what stands in the way.

As so often happens, the important barriers are psychological, and of the sort that could be removed by full understanding. The worker, for example, does not usually sense the importance of capital in his life, nor trace it to its source in his thinking. He is easily persuaded that somewhere there is a remote and powerful group known as the rich who seek to exploit his labor, and he assumes of course that "they" could and should provide all the facilities required in his world. He doesn't see why, for instance, "they" don't buy some decent railroad cars instead of those old coaches he has to ride to work in, and it is hard to explain that he is "they."

One of the most familiar happenings in a steel plant is for a man to come to his foreman and say, "I'd like to get a job for my boy." But probably seldom does the foreman make what is really the right answer. He ought to say, "That's a good kid you've got, Joe, but here is the trouble. It costs the company now about $25,000 to buy the machinery for each new man to use who goes to work, and they haven't got the money.

They used to get it out of earnings, but now that goes for taxes. But if you want to put in your own savings, and get the rest of the gang to put theirs in, the company will give you stock for it, and use the money to buy machinery so your kid can have a job." In the old days this was the way it was done, for it was the ambition of every man's life to work hard and save enough money to set his son up in business, but the vastness of our plants blinds him to its modern counterpart, the purchase of the company's common stock.

And, unhappily, the average employee, even at a high level of ability, is inhibited from doing this because he doesn't know how to. He has never met a man who sells stock, nor seen his place of business. Shares are not sold in a grocery or tavern, and almost never in a mill town by any method. Members of the stock exchange are fully aware of this and eager to enter this market, but so far not all their ingenuity has been able to devise the right merchandising program, or one that will carry itself on a profit basis. If the employee feels awakening interest and talks to the man in the bank, he will probably get a lifting of the eyebrows and a suggestion that a savings account is the right answer. And if he talks to an officer of the company he may do little better, for the low percentage of officials and supervisors who buy the common stocks of their companies is shocking. They buy new automobiles and television sets as their earnings increase, but not common stocks. As their future has grown more secure through the development of pension plans, they have tended more to spend up to the current limit of their salaries, and as a group they show surprising lack of understanding of their own responsibility in perpetuating the plants from which they draw their livelihood.

The best answer that I see to all this is for each company to have a comprehensive program for the offering of its own stock to its employees. By which I mean a plan for all employees, not just the insiders. Payroll deduction solves the mechanics of buying and encourages thrift. And above all such a plan re-establishes a sense of partnership among those whose joint effort carries the enterprise forward. Not only will the mass savings of the workers become available to fill the capital needs for new plants and equipment, but a new means of communication will be opened up between the management and the employees which cannot fail to improve mutual understanding.

Obviously, the whole program must be based upon the voluntary choice of each individual. There must be no employer pressure whatsoever. But there must be explanation. We have for years through war bond campaigns been creating subtly the impression that government securities are the only safe thing in which to invest savings. But an employee must be educated to take the risk of a business investment with his eyes open, to serve his own self-interest.

Unions have for the most part appraised this proposed stockholder relationship correctly, and I know of many militant labor leaders who have bought the common stocks of the companies with which they deal. The outstanding exception — and no one will be surprised — is John L. Lewis. Not long ago, the Wage Stabilization Board, having before it for approval such a company plan, decided for reasons I was never able to fathom, to ask certain labor organizations what they thought of it. For the most part the replies came in promptly and favorably, but the letter from Mr. Lewis was a classic of reactionary nonsense. It contained this sentence: "We believe that such plans do not conform with the traditional principles of the American labor movement and are detrimental to the wage earners in general." Since when did it become detrimental to coal miners to have coal mines made safe, and to have their earnings increased by the use of coal-loading machines to replace the pick and shovel, and electric locomotives instead of mules? And why should any other American put up his savings to bring those things to pass if the coal miner, who will be the first to benefit, is forbidden to put up his? Or does Mr. Lewis mean to imply that the traditional principles of the American labor movement, as he interprets them, are not consistent with the preservation of free enterprise? If so, the quicker we face that question, the better.

When the businessman has convinced his employees that partnership in the enterprise through the purchase of the company's stock is desirable, he would do well to turn his attention to the farmer and seek his partnership as well. The rural areas today offer a second great reservoir of savings that are not being employed as capital for the expansion of industrial plants and the raising of our standard of living. For the first time in a generation, the farmer has cash; the rest of us have seen to that through taxes and parity. But he knows only one ownership, and that is land. The successful farmer has but one primary investment ambition, and that is to buy the adjoining farm. He has thrift but he needs investment diversification. He needs a second basket for his eggs. The mechanical appliances which he is buying so eagerly and which have so transformed his life come to him from a world in which he has no part. Somehow we must find a way to widen his horizons so that he may understand the really simple processes by which savings become industrial capital through the purchase of common stocks, and sense keenly an opportunity to serve his own self-interest thereby.

And there is one further group to whom we might usefully address ourselves to advance understanding of the process of capital accumulation and the profit and loss system under which our production is carried on, but he who puts his ideas in print concerning it runs fearsome risks. I speak of the distaff side. How well I remember the time when I said to a lady, "Do you believe in profit-sharing?" And she replied, "Yes, I'd like to."

No one knows, I suppose, just how large a proportion of the common stock of our companies is owned by women, but it must be very substantial. It is the men who have the coronaries, and the women who take under the will. While we live and are carrying on we don't take much pains to share with her our business philosophy, partly because we are pretty happy-go-lucky about it ourselves, and partly because in mistaken zeal she tries to protect us from ourselves by not letting us talk shop at a social gathering. She thinks the other wives would find very dull a discussion of the distinction between free enterprise and socialism, and she may be right, but those same wives ought to know the difference when they go to the polls to vote. If they don't, they will surely take us down the road toward socialism, since their sensitive awareness of social injustice conditions them to support new ideas dressed up in the disguise of social progress regardless of the impact on the economy. And when they suddenly find themselves fingering for the first time the papers in their deceased husband's safety deposit box they are frightened at their own inexperience in what they classify generically as "legal matters," and cast about for help. They are immensely relieved to find help at hand in the form of the trust department of a bank, and soon their burden is lifted. Thereafter, they receive the monthly remittance from the bank with a list of dividends, which they glance at hastily, but they acquire no understanding by personal experience of the problems of the companies that earn the dividends, and almost none of the threats to the existence of free enterprise itself. They will henceforth regard a proxy as a tiresome document occasionally received in the mail, and an annual report as something that the man in the bank should read. But the man in the bank has hundreds of annual reports to read, and while as a good citizen he may sense a responsibility for fighting the battle to preserve our heritage, he can hardly be expected to multiply his efforts by the number of the widows for whom he acts, or personally carry through the economic education that their husbands neglected. But the ladies, God bless them, go on voting.

It is our responsibility, therefore, as businessmen to explain the significance of the profit system to the members of our families. With women playing increasingly a more important part in the political life of our country, it is our job to help them understand the principles of economic freedom.

CHAPTER VIII The Businessman and
the Universities

WHEN the American businessman arrives at a point in the development of his own philosophy where he is able to emerge from his own environment and look about him with humility he discovers other institutions to which the preservation of freedom is also a passion. He finds that the basic principles upon which he conceives free enterprise to rest have their counterpart in the aspirations of other groups of people, and wistfully he seeks alliance with them, promising himself that he will surely support their cause if they will support his. But they are sometimes suspicious of his motives, and he impatient at their attitudes, and a misunderstanding comes about that blinds both to the urgent need they have of each other in these difficult days.

That is how it is between the businessmen and the educators at present. On the one hand, industry, the

[106]

champion of free enterprise; on the other, the colleges, universities, and other institutions of higher learning, the champions of academic freedom, and between the two groups a widening chasm that most desperately needs to be closed if we are to preserve the America from which both sprang. We businessmen gibe at the visionary schemes of professors "who never met a payroll," and they sneer at the lives of men who worship money. We get a little intemperate on both sides at times, for which we should be compelled to do penance, since nothing could be more certain than that we stand or fall together. The catastrophic struggle going on in the world for the capture of men's minds and souls has reached such a crisis that neither one of us can survive without the other. Our skies are darkening with the clouds that have driven the sunlight of freedom away from both education and business in other lands, and there is no chance that here that sun will continue to shine on one unless it shines on both.

As I see it, freedom is one and indivisible. There are no separate freedoms, but only one heaven-sent quality that must run through every phase of human thought and activity or none, like a high tension wire that goes dead everywhere instantly if severed at one point. Academic freedom and free enterprise are merely different manifestations of the same thing. And it is folly for us not to join hands to preserve it for both of us.

First, let the businessman take a fresh look at the professor. Are we so sure we are always right that we must demand that everyone agree with us, or are we so unsure that we dare not let someone else hold up the mirror and light it brightly that we may see our own defects? We pride ourselves on wanting constructive criticism from our business associates, but we brand it as subversive if it comes from the campus. Actually, each one of us when his anger at a particular professor cools, knows that only by searching differences of opinion do we advance toward truth. Hitler censored thought and destroyed his fatherland.

Then let the professor take a fresh look at the businessman. Freedom to teach what one believes does not require that no effort be made to present to the student body a healthy cross-fertilization of ideas. In the controversial fields of thought such as economics, it would seem to be the obligation of the administration in a university to exercise choice in the selection of the staff in order that the various well-recognized and opposing approaches to the subject might be offered to students by men of equal zeal and capacity. Academic freedom would not seem to require that only men be appointed who teach a planned economy and deficit financing. And it would not seem unreasonable for the businessman who concedes that Fabian socialism should be taught to request that also there be forth-right instruction in free enterprise by a man who understands it. The preservation of balance in view-point within the institution is the key to this dilemma.

And I also think the businessman may reasonably be permitted to wonder why it is that the various programs of economic controls and master-minding that have destroyed freedom for business in many countries, and eclipsed it here, have so often been conceived and executed by professors who in their own campus life fear the loss of freedom for them-selves above all else. How can it be that men who jump at shadows of control 'neath the ivy, leap to the regimentation of businessmen with joy?

But these differences are at the surface, like the sharp words spoken in the family at breakfast, which none of us mean and are all ashamed of. Underneath is the same devotion to a free America, the same deter-mination not to permit our institutions to be engulfed by the madness which has surged across so many lands. Desperately we need each other. We in business need the wisdom and the inspiration of learned men, as have all men through history; we need the annual outpouring of trained young men and women to take up our tasks where we leave off; and we need the priceless achievements of research into both the physical and social sciences which only the universities can undertake. They on the campus need the sturdy financial support of a free economy, lest they be compelled to surrender their own freedom through direct control by the government that meets their deficit. I mean this in no sense as a reflection upon our great state universities, but they remain great because the standards of excellence created by the privately-endowed and altogether independent institutions make it impossible for power-seeking politicians to lay their hands upon them. To preserve an America in which free enterprise may flourish requires that there be forever strong institutions of higher learning maintained by private funds.

This lays a strong obligation on the conscience of the thoughtful businessman, for unless he senses a responsibility to provide support for the colleges and universities no one else will, and their costs have gone up precisely in ratio to his. If he is a college graduate himself he might well be supposed to understand this relationship instinctively, but the record is bad on that. Only a few make annual gifts to their alma maters, and those that do hardly average a sum equal to one month's dues at a country club. And among those to respond to the call of their own beloved campus, not many recognize a second obligation for annual giving to the local college that serves the youth of their area. They give out of sentimentality and nostalgia for what they received, but not out of conviction, or they would want to plow back some of their own good fortune into the soil from which it comes. This creates an imbalance in favor of the older institutions, whereas it is the newer and smaller ones who need help most urgently.

The businessman as a parent is equally disappointing in this matter. He ought to be discerning enough to realize that when he sends his son or daughter to college, and pays the tuition, he has paid only part of the actual cost. The balance is met from income on endowment. In other words, others in earlier years have sacrificed and given their savings to the institution in order that his child might have an education at below cost. Free enterprise could not survive by selling below cost, and he ought to refuse that gift by asking what the true cost is and paying it. For that matter, the institution ought to tell him what the full cost is when they send him the tuition bill, and thus give him an opportunity to make the gift if he is able to, but timidity keeps most of them from doing that.

The women's colleges have perhaps the most difficult time in meeting their budgets because their endowment is always less than that of similar men's institutions. For every hundred dollars of annual giving that a prosperous alumnus undertakes for his alma mater, his wife gives five to hers. And when he dies she feels a sudden and understandable desire to honor his memory by a gift to his college, which usually pre-empts for life her capacity to make a capital gift to her own. When she dies the money goes to the children. Yet it would seem quite clear that in a free America dedicated to equal opportunity, our daughters, the mothers of the next generation, should have the best there is in education.

Having determined the measure of his own personal responsibility for the support of institutions of higher learning, the individual who happens to be a company executive has then to make up his mind what he believes with respect to corporate giving. For myself, I hold that since free universities are vital to the preservation of a society in which free enterprise may flourish, their support is a proper charge upon industry. Since freedom is at stake, let's have done with a legalistic approach to this subject, and do boldly what we know to be right. I doubt that there are laws that stand in the way other than as excuses for selfish men, but if there are, let's change the laws. Let's accept our manifest destiny and throw the support of private industry behind private education with no line drawn between technical studies and the liberal arts. We need fresh insight into the ways of men as urgently as we need new machines, and we need every sort of talent that trained young men and women possess for the carrying forward of our great heritage in the face of our present complexities and hazards.

The corporation which faces up to its broad responsibilities for financial support of community institutions, including those of higher education, soon discovers that it has a difficult administrative problem on its hands, for it requires the same skill to give money wisely that it does to make it. Meetings of boards of directors, limited as they usually are in time, and having agenda top-heavy with formal matters and policy decisions, are not well adapted to the weighing of the relative merits of requests for charitable and educational aid. The more suitable medium is the charitable foundation. Under this plan a separate entity is established with a charter that qualifies it for a tax deduction, into the treasury of which the corporation makes quarterly payments out of income. The Board of Directors of the company determines those amounts, and reviews the list of disbursements annually, but delegates the administrative tasks.

It is the board of the foundation that receives requests and recommendations, both from outsiders and from the company staff, weighs the relative merits of the various proposals, and arrives at decisions. If the group is wisely set up it will include some senior officers whose own participation in community affairs affords a background of rich experience for this delicate task, but also some young men who are just beginning their own community activity, and who may thus receive valuable training. As the work of a new foundation gets under way it proceeds almost necessarily at first by the case method, or cut and try, for the problems of each corporation differ from those of others even in the same industry, but gradually a pattern will develop, and approximate percentages can be set up for such categories as education, hospitals, social agencies, churches, etc. And if the company's board are prudent they will appropriate generously in good years, with the foundation holding to an average level of disbursements, until a reserve has been accumulated that will help to cushion the lean years, thus helping to bring stability to the budgets of the civic institutions.

One very special way by which corporations may bring support to the colleges and universities, and at the same time strengthen their own industrial relations is through the establishment of scholarships for the sons and daughters of employees. This wholesome practice is rapidly growing, and already experience is pointing up certain useful suggestions. Selection of those to receive the awards must be made on such a plane of integrity that there never can be the slightest hint of favoritism, and the best guarantee in that respect is to have the recipients chosen by an outside committee of schoolmen who are paid for that service. Thereafter every step must be taken with the thought in mind that the scholarship holders will make every important decision for themselves, it being citizenship training that we are seeking. They are to name the institution of their choice, from a large accredited list, and are to pursue any course of study they wish, no matter what that may be. It is not for us, for example, to say that metallurgy is important in our modern society but that art is not. Then we communicate with the college chosen, and inquire first what the tuition is, and secondly what the full real cost of the education is. We do not stop by merely paying the tuition, but we send a second check by way of gift to the institution which brings it out whole by our assuming the right share of its total budget. Some companies make this added check identical for all the colleges chosen by students, but I prefer individual gifts that suit each case. By announcing the gift, the college is able to dramatize for its own alumni the fact that tuition is only part of the cost, and to name the exact excess sum required to complete the total.

Research is another area in which the problems of business and those of the universities and the institutes of technology find common ground, and in which each can and should be of assistance to the other. Yet it is still one in which both the possibilities and the obligations are but dimly understood by some businessmen.

For many of us the word research is itself the symbol of the modern magic by which whole industries have been created or transformed overnight, and by which the well-managed company turns out a finer product than its rival. In our advertisements we feature the men in the white coats peering into microscopes to suggest that because we have skilled laboratory scientists our wares are the only safe ones to buy. But we have never boasted that we ourselves have trained those men with the white coats. We like to remind our customers of the graduate degrees they hold, but none of this would be possible if there were not in being great universities and institutes of technology whose job it is to train those scientists upon whose learning and creative skill our prosperity is based. If they are important to production, then the institutions which educate them merit our strong support.

Some of us have the further blind spot that we limit our enthusiasm to applied research, to the finding of a better process that will reduce cost immediately and amortize the expenditure in eighteen months, or to the creation of a better product that will be reflected in increased dividends in the next quarter. Our horizons are too limited for us to realize the vast importance of research that is undertaken with no purpose in view whatever other than the insatiable curiosity of mankind to know the nature of matter or the character of truth: research that is basic, research from which whole new categories of applied uses will ultimately come which no man could foresee at the outset. How many times a whole conflagration in industry has been unexpectedly set off by a spark from scientific inquiries for which no ultimate useful application had even been suggested at the beginning. The basic concepts from which the modern plastics industry has sprung were developed by chemists who were determined to find out why liquids and gases behaved as they did, not by men who were paid to find a new way of making stockings, or a new type of hairbrush.

But there is one further blind spot in the attitudes of businessmen toward research, both applied and basic. When we speak of research we usually mean the physical sciences, the further delving into the mysteries of metals, liquids, and the other forms of matter, and not the social sciences, or the delving into the mysteries of human behavior. Yet what are the problems that cause management the deepest concern today? It isn't products so much as it is people. The things we businessmen worry about most these days cannot be answered by research conducted by physical scientists only. They cannot be measured, or weighed, or tested by instruments, or even seen and felt. They lie within the realm of ideas and that of morals, and must be solved by the processes of reason without physical aids.

We speak glibly of the importance of personnel relations in industry, yet where are the corporations that have made important grants to the social scientists in the universities for research into human behavior? We have learned a great deal about what causes friction in machines, but have not sought to learn what causes friction between human beings. We know what causes heat when metal meets metal, but have not demanded to know what causes heat when man meets man. Physical research has taught us what lubricants to use to reduce friction and heat in machines, but we have established no social research programs to determine what lubricants will best reduce friction among people. Or what do we know about the whole question of mass behavior which breaks out into the riots around our gates, or the broad problem of motivation in human conduct?

Even in the areas that lie midway between the physical and the social sciences, such as health, our support is meager. We spend but paltry sums to determine why men break down, when compared to the vast sums we spend to determine why machines break down. It is common knowledge that half of the executives that die in harness do so because of cardiac or vascular difficulties. Yet how many of our companies are doing anything substantial to determine the causes of heart failure? We keep the most accurate records concerning the down time of our machines, and the interruption in production which they cause, yet who has ever set out to measure the down time of people, the inroads made upon production by cancer, pulmonary difficulties, kidney ailments, gall bladder troubles, and the like? Or take safety. When shall we learn that not all the mechanical guards in the world will prevent an accident if something in the mind or heart of the workman causes him to lapse into doing the wrong thing? And who shall push back the frontier of knowledge with respect to human behavior to the point where we may understand that mystic quality we call leadership, and recognize it infallibly in those whom we employ or promote?

In all such matters the universities stand waiting to serve industry, and if only the educators and the businessman could stop goading one another into recrimination, and rejoice together in the great purposes which they share in common, a new partnership could be brought about that would be of incalculable value to our country, and to the civilization which free men everywhere cherish.

CHAPTER IX Young Men

CONSIDERATION of the problems of the colleges and universities takes one directly to that most absorbing subject of all, the selection and training of young men for responsibility in industry. The businessman who overlooks this important part of his job not only dooms his company to mediocrity in the next generation, but robs himself of one of the deepest satisfactions in life. There is no greater thrill than to choose or promote a young man because he seems to have unusual promise, and then to find this judgment overwhelmingly justified by the experience of the passing years. The men we have picked or advanced provide a much surer index to our own ability than the plants we have built. Most of us spend our own business lives playing on a team we didn't select, and to be thought well of by our successors requires that we do not pass on to them a heritage of personnel blunders.

Selection is too narrow a word to use in the first instance when thinking of building for leadership.

Recognition would be better, recognition and nurturing of unusual ability already existing within the organization. Inside any company in each generation some of the ablest men are never selected: they just get a job anonymously in the old-fashioned way and emerge on merit. The smart boss watches for them and does something about it as soon as they emerge. Some may have formal education, but many will not, and it is still the glory of our country that that doesn't matter. It is staying uneducated that dooms the man, not the starting that way. No man can help it if he has to leave school to support his parents, but he very much can help it if he wants an education thereafter. The thirst for knowledge need never be denied in modern America, and the man who carries his night courses through to completion while doing his full job in the shop in the day has a sense of values and a courage that merit the most thoughtful scrutiny by the boss who is looking for leadership in his organization.

There never are enough such. But as the years pass more and more young men and women from even the lowest income families are able to achieve a formal education, and so the businessman looking for future leadership turns to the various institutions of higher learning. Here the word "select" is used advisedly, for every effort must be made to obtain the best if the company is to excel its competition in the next generation. Aggressive and intelligent recruitment becomes a necessity. It now has a major part in the hot pace of competition. Those companies who rely merely upon recognition of ability among those who apply for jobs will occasionally find a top flight man, but on the average they will be choosing from among those of lesser ability, for among the applicants will be a higher ratio of those who were passed over as mediocre by the active recruiters. A comprehensive plan must resemble the seeded tournament in tennis: the dark horse who wins now and then keeps the play exciting, but there must be seeded players if quality is to be maintained.

How to pick the right group of college seniors for seeding into a company, and what to do with them after they are selected, are fascinating and altogether baffling problems, about which there are as many different viewpoints as there are individual executives who are concerned. I happen to hold strong opinions, but they are strictly personal, and some of my closest friends think I am wrong in many particulars. This variety of approach, however, as among companies even in the same industry is wholesome, and is once more typical of the strength of free enterprise.

To begin with, I am not too happy with the intense zeal of some of the college placement officers who are apt to fall into the habit of mind of scoring their own performance and that of their institution on the basis of the number of seniors whom they place with the so-called good companies. Like the justice of the peace who performs hasty marriages, they sometimes start a train of circumstances that brings unhappiness later. One of their sins, in my opinion, for example, is the coaching they give the boy on the day before he is interviewed by the company representative. Like a horse being groomed for the show ring they want him to appear well for their own sakes or that of the college. So they tell the senior to be crisp and decisive in his answers, and to give the appearance of know-ing his own mind. But how can a boy be wisely crisp and decisive when he is torn by inner doubts and fears? How can a youngster who has never tried to sell anything know that he wants to enter a sales de-partment? Or can he be sure that just because he had a good mark in physics he will do well in production? For myself, I am always wary of the senior who knows his own mind, since I am quite sure that indecision and uncertainty are normal at that time in one's life. The recruiters whom I have trained, therefore, never ask the senior what it is he wants to do, but devote themselves to trying to discover what sort of boy it is they are talking to. And the decisions as to where those selected are to be placed in the company are postponed as long as possible in the training period, to permit the boy to learn all he can about what actually goes on in the company, and the staff to learn all they can about the boy. Complete mutual understanding is a better basis for the future than snap judgment on both sides in March of senior year.

Another fundamental in my creed is that we never select a man for what he knows. It is his capacity to learn that excites me, and particularly his capacity to learn that which he knows nothing about. If he is to be a leader he will spend most of his mature life doing things for which he is not specially trained, and to be effective he must have the intellectual courage and facility to have a go at any problem, no matter how strange. A metallurgist who is afraid of a balance sheet because he had no accounting in college will never rise above the level of technician. Proven competence in some field, plus intense intellectual curiosity and audacity are the essential qualities, it seems to me. The trick is how to detect them in a twenty-minute interview.

Scholastic marks are important. It is of course true that many a man with poor grades comes to great success in later life, usually because his maturing process was slow, but as a matter of cold calculation there will be fewer such among the C's than among the B's, and fewer there than among the A's. Once the intellectual capacity is established, the interviewer can turn to the other desired qualities, but to choose a dull mind because the boy is pleasant is not being fair to the future.

The list of the other qualities must start with character. There is no substitute for character — the awareness of moral problems, and the courage to do the right thing under all conditions of life. The brilliant but dishonest mind and heart may bring disaster to the company in later years, and no young man is worthy who lacks rugged integrity.

Then comes an instinct for human relations. Here is where the intellectual must be watched carefully, for if he is too intent on the processes of the mind to be aware of what people think of him, he will not understand team play in industry.

And then comes the capacity for self-expression. Many a brilliant mind has burned itself out in industry because the man could not communicate to those of lesser intellectual power the advanced ideas which he had conceived. Writing and speaking English clearly and concisely are indispensable as working tools in modern business.

This is not intended as a complete list of qualities that may attract an interviewer, but rather to point up the opinion that I hold that there is no single scholastic discipline or training that is the best preparation for the steel industry, or any other business. Such qualities are to be found among the seniors of every school, and among students of science or students of the liberal arts. It is the qualities that we seek, and not specific knowledge acquired by the student in a particular field of concentration. And if we base our decisions on the qualities, wherever they may be found, we will surely at the same time give our companies a wide variety of educational backgrounds.

Personally, I like a full year of company training for the seeded player before he is assigned to a job, a sort of postgraduate course in the particular affairs of the one institution. This should be as broad as possible, for once he is in a groove it will be many years before the young man can look around again. That year is his own golden opportunity to equip himself with a breadth of background which may thereafter lie fallow until he approaches middle age. He should see not only things but people, and all of the key officials should study him as he studies them. If possible, he should work with his hands and not be merely an observer, but that is very hard to accomplish as he moves from department to department, since he cannot remain long enough to receive the necessary training. At any rate, he should live in the plant community, and be urged to seek every opportunity of forming friendships with employee families. If the trainees form a group, they should be encouraged to take their meals together in order that the bull session may be continuous. The cross-currents of comment that flow back and forth between the technically trained and those from the liberal arts are very humbling and very salutary on both sides, and as mutual respect develops comradeships are formed that mean a great deal in future years.

Actual placement at the end of the training year is seldom difficult. The first to be weeded out are those occasional ones who find neither the industry nor the company to their liking, and much later heartache will be avoided if such are encouraged to leave without the slightest feeling of moral obligation for the year of training. Those who remain are the keen ones who sense that this is precisely the company they want to work for, and who now are so well informed about the whole organization that they want to try out for a particular job. The indecision of senior year has given way to confidence born of knowledge and experience.

Occasionally, there is the black sheep who casts discredit on his generation and breeds cynicism in the heart of his boss — the boy who signs on with his tongue in his cheek, never intending to stay permanently, but planning deliberately to steal two or three more years of training and then sell his services in the market of those employers who are too lazy to provide training. The dishonesty lies in the fact that he permits himself to be overpaid during the early years, and leaves before he has pulled his weight.

Once the boy is placed the real battle begins, and it is one that tries the soul of the most understanding executive. Seeded players are temperamental, whether on the tennis courts or in industry, and to bring the unusual young man safely through the restiveness of his first five years is a ticklish task in human engineering. To begin with, his immediate superior will probably not be helpful. If he is not a college man himself, he may resent college men. If he happens to have one of the slower minds, he resents the facile speech and mental quickness of the boy who led his class. Having come up the hard way himself, he withholds information and assigns the newcomer repetitive tasks that fill him with dismal boredom. And the understanding boss must bite his fingernails through all this, for if he so much as inquires about the youngster he gives the kiss of death to his advancement on merit. It must always be clear that the boy is not teacher's pet, and he must have no promotion that has not been won in competition with all comers, or where his ability has not been fully recognized by all concerned. Only the boy himself can lick the problem, and he does it by infinite patience, an honest smile, and faith in his own future.

About a third of them can't take it, however, and jump during the first five years. They become morbidly convinced that they have been forgotten, that they are getting nowhere, and that the road ahead is too long for them to endure. In college they found fresh intellectual challenge as they began each new course, and to perform the same task each day for even six months in industry establishes a boredom in their lives which soon exhausts their scant supply of patience. So they walk out, and the man who came up the hard way smiles knowingly at the worthlessness of the youngsters of today.

Almost invariably they jump to small companies, proud of the fifty-dollar-a-month increase which the new employer is glad to give them because it has saved him the trouble of recruiting, and buoyed up with hope that soon they will have genuine responsibility. And usually that happens. It is ordinarily true that in the early years young men advance more rapidly both in compensation and in authority in small companies than in so-called big business. Larger organizations with well-developed personnel programs protect themselves in depth with talent so far as possible, and not only have substitutes in the line of succession, but substitutes for the substitutes. The ultimate target is the thing, however, and that is something which is very difficult to explain to a young man about to be married to whom an immediate pay increase is the most important thing in life. Vaguely he thinks that at forty he will be eagerly sought after and that he will then go back to a fine job in a large institution, but it seldom works out that way. Large companies go outside for talent only as a last resort and because someone failed in their personnel planning, for they must reward those who didn't jump. And nothing makes an older man more heartsick than to watch through the years the career of a boy who jumped, and find him eventually stymied in a job too small for him, just because economic circumstances doomed his company to stagnation. And to talk to him before he leaves about the greater security to be found in a large organization is wasted effort that he sits through with reluctance, for what is to happen to him at sixty-five has less gravitational pull with him than the moon has on a millpond.

But over the years — and this process in one form or another has been going on for a long time — these jumpers, the seeded players who leave the large companies to sign on with the small, have had a marked influence on our economy. No one who has sat as I have on boards of business and civic organizations made up of men drawn from every section of the country and all industries can have failed to observe with some chagrin that the brilliant creative minds and the courageous natural leaders seem to be found more often in the smaller companies than in the large. I am afraid that this is a process of natural selection. Too many men who dare, jump, and eventually a man who didn't have the courage to leave becomes president of the large institution by seniority, simply because he was there. So the problem of the large companies is to find a way to bring the seeded players, the would-be jumpers, the men of spark and audacity through the restive period into the tranquility of recognized opportunity.

This requires subtlety and an ever-watchful eye on the part of the top management. One useful technique is what I like to call horizontal promotion, by which the promising man, whether a seeded player or one who came up the hard way, is not kept too long on one job or in one sequence. He will do much to train himself for future responsibility if given the chance, but unusual ability, like a fine machine, must be tuned up by use. The larger the company the greater degree of specialization, and if that process is not resisted it will give the company of the future a magnificent group of technicians with no one qualified to direct them. The breadth of judgment required of a seasoned executive at middle life is a function of experience, but the man of promise can acquire that experience only if his boss consciously makes it possible.

Similarly the experience in civic responsibility which these future leaders must have if the free enterprise system is to be perpetuated can be made possible only by conscious stimulation and intelligent recognition on the part of the senior executives. No longer may they gibe at the patriotic youngster who wants to serve in the National Guard: "What's the matter, haven't you got enough to do around here?" On the contrary, they must suggest the names of likely juniors to civic organizations who are recruiting workers, and go out of their way to compliment those who volunteer for such assignments. Likewise they must watch for signs of the articulate quality, and encourage the youngsters to try their wings at speaking about their own fields of interest to church groups, luncheon clubs, etc. Above all, they themselves must set a worthy example in all these things.

There is one habit which we older men have in dealing with employment which I deplore, but I must confess that in holding my opinions I find myself in a most exclusive minority. Actually, the attitude of which I complain is a piece of unreasoned folklore that is commonly accepted and practiced because, in my view, it is not thought through. These are the usual circumstances. In even those companies that for years have been outstanding in their personnel planning and administration there come emergencies. Perhaps the number two in a sequence resigns, and the senior suffers a coronary, all in the same month, leaving a key spot without coverage, and creating a situation so desperate that the management has no alternative but to go outside for a replacement. There isn't time to bring in a junior by lateral transfer and give him the necessary training, for immediate experience is demanded at a mature level. Invariably under those conditions the management casts covetous eyes on the number two in the same sequence in the organization of a strong competitor, and the question arises of whether the consent of that company should be secured before the man is approached. The accepted code is that such consent must always be obtained, and that the matter should be dropped if the other company demurs.

Personally I do not consider myself bound by that code, nor do I ask others to respect it in dealing with me, for it seems to me that the practice plainly violates the freedom of individual action which we are seeking so earnestly to preserve. Who am I to decide for one of my subordinates a matter which vitally touches his whole life? He is entitled to make his own decisions as to whether the opportunity offered by the other company is greater than that of his present prospect, and it is not in keeping with our concept of the worth of the individual in a democracy to bargain about him like a piece of merchandise without his knowledge. If he leaves our company, and I am unhappy, it would indicate that we have underpaid him, or withheld from him an insight into the future to which he was entitled. So I hire the competitor's man if I want to, and make no preliminary telephone call.

And there is then one final phobia that I have about young men in which again I am sadly in the minority, though again I like to think that the conventional attitude receives wide acceptance because the individual executives do not pause to think it through. It has to do with industrial deferment from military service. Beginning in my war back in 1917, and coming strongly into favor in the last war, as well as in the successive crises since 1945, has been the concept that the chemist, the metallurgist, the engineer, and the other technically trained students must not bear arms. They constitute a special reserve of brains which the nation must not jeopardize. They are to stay in the factories and devise new weapons while the liberal arts boys do the dying. Yet from among those same impractical students of the humanities and the social sciences might come the future Churchills, the men of ideals and character, who would hold aloft the torch of leadership in their country for either war or peace. So I cannot think it is just to have a planned economy in death. The grim burden should be shared by all alike.

But I must close this chapter as I began it by paying my respect once more to the youth in American industry today, and expressing my warm affection for them. They are magnificent, and the question is not whether they will fail us, but rather whether we will fail them.

CHAPTER X The Businessman and
Foreign Policy

THE WHOLE SERIES of foreign problems in which the
United States is involved is a subject about which the
average businessman has probably the least personal
experience from which to form a working set of
opinions. And yet this happens to be one of the few
subjects upon which he often does express himself, and
with violence, in his desire to contribute to the public
thinking in his own community. One would hesitate
to believe that the articulate quality is exercised in reverse ratio to knowledge and understanding, yet this
curious phenomenon seems to point in that direction.
Listen in on any railway lounge car conversation, or
during any trade association luncheon, and it will be
made clear that as a group we know a great deal about
the foreign policy of our country. Otherwise, how
could we be so universally sure that it is wrong in its
entirety?

Yet seldom do we really know what we are talking about, and least of all could we agree as a group upon what the right policy should be. Some would say that we never should have gone into Korea, and others that we never should have pulled out. We pretty much are together in wanting resistance offered to communism, but there must be no dollar aid to any nation that is not grateful. We must not interfere in the internal affairs of other countries, but on the other hand we surely must not give dollar aid except where it will promote free enterprise and block socialism. For a time it was popular to say that instead of dollars we should export our know-how, but when a request is made to borrow an expert for service overseas, his job is so important that he can't be spared. We condemn the wasteful incompetence of the bureaucrats who are spending our tax money on visionary schemes, but when in good faith we are urged to close our own desks temporarily and accept posts of responsibility where we can direct the spending ourselves, we want no part in it. When we hear of a competitor doing it we say, "What in the world would he want to go to Greece for?", and add dryly that he never was much good in the business anyway. Or else that he always was a publicity hound.

Actually these attitudes are proof of an ignorance, the existence of which we are loath to admit. For example, it is rather surprising how many top executives of American companies there are who have never been outside the United States, let alone have command of a foreign language, or read consistently a foreign periodical, or entertain in their homes their opposite numbers from overseas industry. They have no bench marks of their own to which they may tie opinions, and no correctives for those which they absorb unconsciously from the radio, the club, and the newspapers. A little knowledge may be a dangerous thing, but in dealing with our foreign problems it quickly brings humility, and closes many mouths.

I ought to know, for I was one of the most ignorant when in 1948 Mr. Paul Hoffman suddenly catapulted me into Paris as the first steel consultant to Mr. Averell Harriman just as he was setting up the E.C.A. staff for the administration of the Marshall Plan. I had happened to hear General Marshall deliver his now famous address at the Harvard Commencement in that year, but it was just another pretty good speech so far as I was concerned, and I went happily along to my class reunion without the slightest awareness that he had said anything which in any way concerned me. I was neither for nor against the Marshall Plan nor anything else that had to do with foreign policy. My job was in Chicago, and in great confidence I would have been prepared to admit that it was a pretty important one, certainly one I couldn't think of leaving for a public assignment no matter how worthy. I had spent a little time in France in the first war, and had been back as a tourist with my family, but I had no further plans for going back, at least before I retired. As for steel, I couldn't have told with certainty what countries produced it, and, of course, didn't know the name of a single company, nor had I met a single individual connected with the industry. I was a typical self-satisfied American businessman.

But suddenly there I was, plunged up to my neck in the Marshall Plan. Mr. Harriman didn't know what my job was, but asked me to find out and come back and tell him, a statement that seemed completely preposterous to me at the time, but one which soon began to make sense. How could he know? How could anyone know? I began to wake up, and to realize that I had the great opportunity of being present when the American government embarked upon a vast project that could destroy our economy if it were not wisely administered; and that if I were unable to make a sound contribution out of my business experience, in analyzing the problem and making specific proposals, I must never again scream at the bureaucrats. So I did try to find out and tell Mr. Harriman what I thought the relationship of the Marshall Plan was to steel.

The deeper I dug and the harder I worked the more humble I became, as I came to grips with the world problem at first hand. Often I wanted to quit because for the life of me I couldn't make up my mind what I ought to advise the bureaucrats to do if they were to let me write the whole ticket. I came to know too much to be sure any more. And, so, since my term ended I have been back several times, and the friendships I formed in the various countries have deepened. I have visited my opposite numbers, and they have been my guests in Chicago. We exchange letters constantly. At past middle life I have achieved fair competency in the French language. My Continental friends can thus write me in that language, while I reply in English. And I read each week one French magazine and the *London Economist*, so that I know at first hand what foreigners think of American policies. That, of course, is not always a pleasant experience. From all of this I have painfully evolved the nucleus at least of a working set of opinions.

I start with the thought that whether we like it or whether we don't the United States is in the center of world affairs. The question is no longer whether we should be there but rather how we shall conduct ourselves in the face of the obvious fact that there we are. I leave to the historians the debate as to whether the circumstances under which these vast new global obligations, both moral and economic, under which we stagger could have been escaped by following this or that course as each new crisis developed, and propose to limit my soul-searching to the perplexities from here on. Sufficient unto my day is that evil. And in terms of the preservation of free enterprise it seems to me high time that the businessman plunge into this morass, for the world turmoil has reached a point where a decision made in Europe, the Near East, or the Orient by an American may have more impact on the future of a business in Kankakee than any the ablest president in the world could make with respect to the internal affairs of his company. In our own self-interest we can no longer afford to yield these battles by default, merely to enjoy the pleasures of invective thereafter.

This was how my mind worked when I found myself without either warning or training in the midst of the Marshall Plan. I had had no part in establishing our national policy, not even that of the ordinarily prudent citizen, for you will search my files in vain to find a single letter to a member of either house in Congress written to protest global spending between the time when I listened to General Marshall at the Harvard Commencement and the day nearly a year later when I received my telephone call from Mr. Hoffman. Nor for that matter will you find them in the files of those of my friends who are now the most critical of the program. They and I walked out on the whole question of postwar Europe, and left it to the bureaucrats.

When I flew the Atlantic with trepidation for the first time and arrived at the Paris headquarters of E.C.A. just as the plasterers were finishing our temporary offices, and when there was only one telephone for six of us industrial specialists to use, I accepted the fact that there was already established by my country a revolutionary policy of breath-taking proportions, and I made up my mind that since it was my dollars that were being spent I would do what I could to prevent waste and make the administration of the plan as efficient as possible. And I have been at that ever since. When I have felt that mistakes were being made — and there have been many such occasions — I have addressed myself to those in charge and not to the man in the street, because I have never felt that I could contribute to any discussion by walking angrily out of the room.

I have come rather soberly to the conviction, however, that no President of the United States, whether Democrat or Republican, could have failed to take some emergency action in Europe at the close of the war. The risks were too great to hazard the gamble that nothing would come of them. However one might have hoped and prayed that Russia would live at peace with her neighbors, and above all that she would never launch a direct attack on our country, an overpowering sense of responsibility to future generations would have driven any man to the decision that doubts must be resolved in favor of American security. A hostile Russia based behind the Elbe would be menace enough, but how could anyone doubt that if Russia should dash to the Atlantic, as the Germans had, she would be a far greater menace? Who could have taken that risk lightly, or who could have lived with his conscience if he had not determined to stop it? Take steel, for example, the basic commodity in modern warfare. Had Russia swept through the Ruhr, picking up on her way the neighboring steel districts in Holland, Belgium, France, and Luxemburg, and neutralizing those of England by her proximity from channel ports, we would have handed her as much war potential in steel as half of all that we ourselves then possessed, and I for one would have thought that too great a risk to take. Having kept the western European steel industry on our side, we outpoint Russia and her satellites more than three to one. When I think of my grandchildren, I like it better that way.

And I am also driven rather soberly to the conviction that the Marshall Plan turned the trick. If so, it was cheap insurance against a new loss in American lives and capital, unwise as may have been some of its policies, and bad as may have been its administration in some particulars. I have come to believe that the mere announcement of the program, while it was still only a gleam in General Marshall's eye, was sufficient to snatch Italy back from communism, and if Italy had been lost how could France have been saved, and beyond that I refuse to speculate. If E.C.A. did that much I am sure it was right to try, but, of course, I know it did far more. It brought hope to the hearts of those within the bleeding, bankrupt, devasted areas that someone would stand at their sides if they would struggle; and, although in the years that have passed some of those men have often tried our patience sorely, as they have the patience of each other, we may be very sure that the astonishing degree of recovery already achieved has caused much grinding of the teeth in the Kremlin. No honest-minded businessman can fail to sense that American security, and that alone is the test, has been advanced in the past five years; and the question now before us is how and where to stop before it comes tragically to pass that this security has been purchased at the cost of permanent impairment of the soundness of our economy. We must weigh that equation objectively as businessmen and as Americans, but to do so we must equip ourselves with understanding of the risks, both those that have been faced and those that remain.

Once we adopt the hypothesis that American aid to Europe is justified for no other purpose than to advance American security, much that has been confused in our thinking can be cleared up. Take the gratitude argument, for example. People say, "But are they grateful?" Well actually they aren't, in the sense that the question is asked. Here and there among thoughtful citizens of the various E.C.A. countries an American sometimes encounters a warmth of sentiment that goes straight to his heart, and on public occasions and in public documents there are gracious references to the unprecedented generosity of our country, but speaking broadly the criticism is more true than false. The European man in the street neither knows nor cares what we have done, and to the extent that he does understand he is easily persuaded either that it was his just due because of his own sacrifice in war, or that we are doing it for evil motives. But if we are there merely to serve ourselves and advance our own security, this is no reason for abandoning the program. It is merely a circumstance that adds to our difficulty.

That there is lack of understanding on the other side is not to be wondered at. We ourselves have been inept at times in our overseas public relations: you can't sell gratitude in Italy as you sell soap in Brooklyn. And oddly enough, politicians in other countries are quite like our own in wishing to destroy the myth of Santa Claus and announce themselves as the ones who brought the presents. The party in power invariably takes the credit for improvement of conditions in all countries, regardless of the true cause, and therefore we have had little help in arousing gratitude anywhere. As for the businessman over there, his is a special case, and it is strictly true that he has received no gifts. Some people seem to be under the impression that when a new mill for the continuous rolling of steel is built in France after a grant from E.C.A., the company which is to operate it receives it without paying for it, but that is a complete misconception. The dollar grant which makes possible the buying of the heavy machinery in this country goes to the French government, but the steel company acquires the equipment only after it provides for the cost out of its own capital, either by depositing francs, or its corporate obligations, with its government. Thus are provided the counterpart funds one reads about, but they are just as real with the steel company over there as a bond issue would be with us.

At the root of much of the difficulty in the wise administration of a program like the Marshall Plan, or for that matter in the forming of intelligent American opinion on any of the great questions of the day in the field of foreign relations, is the barrier of communication, and the chasm in ideas and attitudes that divides America from her new neighbors by a distance which psychologically is as great as that of the ocean which divides us geographically. Try as we will, we simply do not understand one another. Nor do I mean language here. I wish very much that each American businessman had at his command some second language, as most of his European opposite numbers do, but this goes far deeper than that. If we all spoke English or French fluently we still wouldn't understand one another.

Take capitalism or free enterprise, for instance. Those words even when correctly translated do not convey the same meaning to the minds of listeners on the other side of the Atlantic that they do to us. Nor does the word competition. The European concept of production under private management stops far short of that which enlightened industrial leadership considers to be the ideal for this country, and clings to attributes which we have rejected. These areas of difference have deep significance as we grope our way toward unity of thought and action in the Western world, and so far as I know they have never been intelligently explored. It would be a fertile field for scholarly study in a day when we are seeking to break down the barriers to better understanding of the peoples of the world, and a great contribution could be made by business if some of our foundations would undertake a comprehensive study in this field.

Actually the European businessman rejects price competition and the free market completely. In fact, in some of the languages there is no single word by which our concept can be expressed. In French, for example, the word for competition is "concurrence," which carries the obvious connotation that the normal relationship between men in the same industry is mutual agreement on all matters, instead of rivalry. One very distinguished European industrialist, for whom I have great respect and affection because of the radiant and courageous quality of his leadership, pleaded with me to listen to him for one hour without interruption in order that he might lead me out of American barbarism, and bring me into the light where I would see that there should be competition on quality and service always, but price never. This universal instinct for group action goes beyond the desire for price agreements, and leads into production quotas, allocations of territory, and the "rationalization" of an industry so that no company will intrude upon the field of specialization staked out by another.

How I abhor that word "rationalization," which is the new euphemism so widely current, employed to gloss over the infinite capacity of European ingenuity in designing ways to bilk the consumer and avoid the risks of rugged free enterprise. In other words, it isn't collectivism that they oppose so much as it is collectivism by government. If they may be the collectivists they love it. But it seems to me desperately clear, both in theory and in the light of recent history, that one leads directly to the other, and that there is no middle ground between the freedom and risk of our way on the one hand, and the security of group action that leads to socialism on the other. Surely no free people will long hereafter tolerate private group action that adversely affects the general welfare, and even though the intentions be as beneficent as though the authors were all saints, the power to suspend natural laws is such a threat to the well-being of society, that it cannot safely be placed in private hands.

This is a difficult subject to debate with one's European friends for the further reason that they do not for one minute believe that we mean what we say. They think we have our tongues in our cheeks about the virtues of competition, and that we would leap glee-fully on their bandwagon if we were not kept in line by the fact that we live in daily fear of our anti-trust laws. Europe has no Sherman Act or Clayton Act, for which they consider themselves thrice blessed, and they fancy us as secretly envious of their state of bliss. We must demonstrate therefore by our conduct that we honestly believe in the free market, law or no law, and one way in which that is being effectively done is through the example being set by some of our leading companies in their overseas subsidiaries. Fortunately, Americans are practising what they preach in Europe: they are risking large sums of capital and doing a magnificent job of improving quality and lowering prices in total disregard of all attempts to bring them into the lodge.

Nor have the traditional industrial leaders of Europe, particularly those of the hereditary-owner groups, recognized that the world is on the march in the matter of passing on to the worker part of the fruit of increased productivity in the form of higher wages. There are still too many companies where the worker tips his cap in fealty as the master walks through the plant just before taking off for his villa on the Riviera. There is still too wide a gap in income between the very rich, and the worker, and something must be done about it before the general standard of living can rise. But like all hasty criticism leveled at Europe by the American businessman who tours a half-dozen countries quickly in his hired Cadillac — and this is a favorite one — there is another side. The thoughtful man in those industries will say to you that the most imperative need of all is for new capital with which to bring on a great expansion of production facilities such as we have experienced, and that in the face of war devastation and war debts there is no source of new capital except retained earnings. He honestly believes that the worker will profit most in the long run if he will be patient a little longer in the matter of wages, and permit the labor-saving devices to be procured through which all consumer prices can be brought down. Perhaps the truth lies in between these extremes, but if when the new plants are finished the prices do not in fact come down, we shall know that our friends in European management have not abandoned their earlier ways.

Some American businessmen would solve the problem very neatly: they would write the ticket and attach it to our dollars. They would make it a condition of economic aid that each country carry through the reforms that we would dictate. Not infrequently this attitude is expressed with appropriate profanity and table thumping. But what an unthinkable responsibility that would be! Who are we to tell any other nation what way of life it should follow, particularly when the form it has chosen was arrived at by democratic processes and after free elections? Take socialism in England, for example. I was often criticized for having had some small part in Marshall Plan activities that tended to support a Labor government with which I was in complete disagreement ideologically. But that government had been freely chosen by secret ballot of the people, and I came back to my basic philosophy that we were in Europe for no other reason than to advance our own security, and that a strong Britain was essential to that security. I thought that the nationalization of steel was a catastrophe, but if our concept of freedom of choice means anything, the British people are certainly entitled to decide that as they wish. It does make our job of promoting our own security more difficult, but if we quit because of that then we never should have started, which could only mean that we were wrong in thinking that our security was threatened.

In honest truth many American businessmen who signed on with E.C.A. for temporary duty were too brittle on this and smiliar matters to be effective in their jobs. They wanted direct and immediate action on debatable questions, and lacked the personal experience to sense the psychological barriers that lay between them and the proud peoples with whom they dealt, barriers that had their origins centuries ago, and that no amount of American technical know-how or aggressiveness could eliminate overnight. Sometimes, too, there was the sad spectacle of an executive who for years had been made to look smart at home by an alert staff, but who standing on his own in a strange environment and facing new situations wasn't a match for the bureaucrats whom he despised.

With the businessman's skepticism as to Point Four, I have the strongest sympathy. It's a Mad Hatter's race at best. No immediate gain in our own security can be achieved by bringing the refrigerator to the jungle, and what shall it profit us if we save the world and destroy ourselves? But what seems to me the most compelling consideration seldom shines through our verbal barrages. It won't work, and our billions will be wasted for lack of an existing entrepreneurial class in the backward countries. If risk-taking for gain is the hard core of dynamism in our economy, then it is folly to dump capital into areas where no group exists who will know what to do with it. The missionary and the teacher must precede the production specialist.

But with the businessman's off-the-cuff method of handling the prickly cactus of trade with the lands under communist control, which is simply to prohibit it altogether by law, always direct and immediate, the case is not so clear. We in the steel industry have in the past received a good deal of manganese and chrome from Russia, commodities which the United States does not possess in quantity, and, as to which, it has not been easy to find alternate sources. Obviously whoever receives must give in exchange. Western Germany has through all history received her cereal grains from the Ukraine, and if she is to buy there now, she must pay. If we want to take her off the back of the American taxpayer we must let her earn her food by exchanging for it the product of her own goods and services. Sweden has no coal within her boundaries, and we must not charge her with communist sympathies just because she buys Polish coal to heat her homes and bunker her vessels, and pays for it with iron ore, even though that gives a much needed and vital raw material to the enemy and takes it from our allies. I am not arguing for no barriers at all, since security is at stake, but I do suggest that there are no easy solutions to problems of such complexity, and that we in business need to approach them with a touch of humility, and take some time to think them out.

Then out of the current maelstrom of foreign affairs has come a new word that will be widely current soon in the field of industrial relations which, because of its obvious pertinence, all of us would know about if we had the habit of mind of following developments in other lands. It is "co-determination." This is the approximate English equivalent of a German word which expresses the postwar demand of the labor unions in Western Germany that they be given a veto power with respect to all management decisions. In steel they asked for equal representation on company boards of directors, and were granted it, the only slender thread of protection left to the owners being an elaborate mechanism for choosing the odd man on a board of eleven. Since American labor leaders went to Germany and had an active hand in bringing this to pass, and since at least one national convention of one of our large unions has already endorsed it, we may safely assume that we shall hear more of it. The same American labor leaders are already engaged in trying to spread the pattern in Europe. They seem to understand that what happens over there can be important here. But on the management side we still have our eyes closed.

I am quite ashamed to toss off such vast problems in such casual phrases, but after all I am not attempting to do more than outline the present state of my own thinking. I am merely trying to advance the thesis that we in business must begin to come to grips with foreign problems because the impact they are making on our daily business lives is growing in its directness and intensity, and if the views which I have expressed are unacceptable, they may at least stimulate others to form their own, and that is my real target.

CHAPTER XI Retirement

It is always high adventure for me when I am privileged to stand in the pilot house of a great steamer plying in the iron ore trade on the Great Lakes, with the blue sky above and the blue of Lake Superior all around, and to watch silently the skillful manipulation of the vessel. It is the job of the wheelsman to keep her on her course, and he does that not only by watching the compass and looking ahead, but by an occasional look over his shoulder to see what her wake is like, the trail left in the water by her rudder and propeller.

It is like that with a business life. As a man comes toward the end of his active participation in the affairs of industry it is fitting that he should pause for a look over his shoulder at his own wake. He will have come through many storms and some spells of good sailing, and it is proper that he should ask himself what the throb of his propeller has been like, and what the angle of his rudder. Perhaps he has turned too many revolutions to the minute, or perhaps not enough, and maybe he has wasted power by too many nervous changes of direction. In any event, he should know, for in retirement there will still be years ahead in which to make compensations for previous errors.

I suppose that one of the first thoughts that occurs to an older man as he takes this look over his shoulder is to marvel at how little his life has resembled the plan that he so carefully formed during senior year in college or when he took his first job. For myself, I happen to be doing nothing for which I was trained, certainly nothing that I had planned or even dreamed about when in college, and yet no one could be happier in his vocation. Isn't it more often that way than not? Don't most businessmen ultimately find themselves on a course that wasn't on the chart when their ship left port? Just at random I think of a mining engineer who sold automobile batteries, an apothecary who became president of a mining company, and an accountant who managed industrial relations for a large corporation. So when young men come to see me during the Christmas holidays of senior year in college, and I find them tense and worried for fear they will take the wrong job, I urge them to relax and take a free swing at the ball. I know that however carefully they plan they will wind up doing something else. Unpredictable circumstances will take a hand and shove their lives this way or that, as has happened so often with the rest of us, and there is no single best way to begin. Any one of a dozen ways that look good can be chosen, and then the course can be charted from the new landmarks that will appear as the ship picks up speed.

The businessman at the senior level looking back will sense that life has brought him many deep satisfactions. There may be a new product he designed which has given comfort or pleasure to many people, or a new plant which he has built which has brought new prosperity to an undeveloped area, or men whom he has promoted who have abundantly established the wisdom of his choice, or an idea which he has expressed forcibly which has had wide acceptance and contributed to the advance of sound business thinking. And then there are the offsets. He will remember the noisy quarrels he had that now seem so petty, the issues he espoused where later he saw that he was on the wrong side, the men whom he called stupid or stuffy for whom he later came to feel deep respect and affection, and the heartache he felt when with tight lips he reached the conclusion that organizational changes had to be made that brought unhappiness to old friends.

And conscious of his own limitations he comes to ponder on the generic limitations of the management group as a whole. Just as the captain of a lake freighter sees other ships on the horizon that seem to be slightly off course, and wonders whether he is right, or they, so the senior businessman looks at his contemporaries. Having in mind his own keen desire to help mould the characters of his juniors and guide the development of their talents, he would like to inventory the commendable qualities that he finds in business leadership generally, and to weigh them against the limitations.

One of the weaknesses that distress me is the unwillingness of some executives to have an opinion of their own on a new problem until they know what someone similarly placed in another company thinks about it. This is not leadership. A man must be a broadcasting station and not just a receiving set. But it is hard to resist the impulse to grab the telephone and ask what some other fellow did before making up one's own mind about the right or wrong of the proposal. Often that other man is himself the same sort of mental and moral procrastinator, and the opinion he gives may have been likewise arrived at by his having grabbed the telephone to call still another. And so it comes to pass that if the first man who had to face up to the question chose the wrong course, his error will be magnified many times until the error becomes policy for an entire industry. To check with one's contemporaries after arriving at one's own decision tentatively is the most obvious sort of prudence, but to check first as a substitute for thinking is not the stuff of which leadership is made.

Genuine delegation of authority is another area of administration where it is difficult to make practice conform to theory. Every student of business, every professional in the field of management engineering, in fact every businessman of mature experience knows that the secret of effective organization lies in the wise distribution of duties among many, their work being guided and coordinated by a supervisor who refrains from performing the tasks himself, and that this is delegation of authority. Most of us seniors labor under the delusion that we do this well, but I am afraid that we are often mistaken.

I know a man who honestly believes that this is one of his strong points, but this is the situation as I have it from one of his associates. On Monday he calls in a subordinate, explains the problem, and tells him to get into it at once; on Tuesday he delegates it to another; on Wednesday he does the job himself and tells neither of the others that he has acted. I know another executive who delegates all right — he never does anything himself if it can be avoided — but never in accordance with any discernible pattern; it is usually the first man he meets as he walks down the hall to whom he hands the file. Often a corporate officer delegates eagerly the things he dislikes, no matter how important, and keeps those that interest him, no matter how trivial. If a man likes purchasing he is apt not to trust his buyer, if he is a chemist by profession he clears his desk of financial matters but keeps his hand on research, if he was once a lawyer he isn't sure the company is employing the right counsel, but would put trust at once in an engineer whom he knows little about. There is one final test, however, in my opinion by which it can be determined whether an executive is objective and consistent in the practice of delegating authority, and that is this: if he can turn a job over to a junior and then support him in carrying it out in a manner quite different from that which he him-self would have chosen, then he understands.

Many other impressions begin to take definite shape

in the mind of the man who is looking back as bearing upon the qualities of administrative ability and business leadership, impressions that he has been but dimly aware of because he has so seldom paused to reflect upon the significance of what was happening about him, and I mention the foregoing merely as illustrations of observations that can become a part of one's personal philosophy. But one experience transcends all others, testing to the full whether the wake has been straight and the course based on accurate bearings, testing whether the individual has fully established a scale of values in his life, and calling for high courage as well as clarity of thought. That experience is retirement.

What a welter of contrary thinking is to be found today on this delicate but important subject, not only among businessmen, but among economists, students of the theory of administration, psychologists and sociologists. Clearly we must know much more about it, and continue the debate much further before general agreement can emerge as to what is right, but it is something each of us older men ought to swim into, instead of just drifting. Most obviously we ought to know what we believe, and why. Solely to make my own contribution to the debate, I shall try to put down my own convictions. At the moment, I feel certain that I am right, but I have felt that way before when it turned out that I was wrong. And I shall limit my comment to the retirement of officials in larger publicly owned companies, for there are obvious special considerations in dealing with the professions and family businesses, and since I am concerned here with a philosophy for executives, I will not discuss retirement for the worker.

One thing I note. Among junior executives at about the age of forty there is never any doubt but that there should be compulsory and complete retirement for older men at not later than the age of sixty-five. The doubts come to those who have passed sixty, and the subtle self-hypnosis of indispensability seems to be associated with thinning hair, bifocals, dentures, and longer belts. It is the occupational disease of seniors.

I am convinced that for purposes of sound administration there must be a fixed age limit with compulsory retirement from active day-to-day responsibility, as distinguished from wisdom duties such as membership on a board of directors. I will try to explain why in a moment, but first let me set the age. For the wisdom jobs I would make it seventy; for the deciding jobs, sixty-five. As to either category, I recognize that medical science is rapidly extending the useful span of life, and that experience might permit either of those limits to be lifted somewhat, but I do not believe that time has yet come. I think the Congress was right when it established sixty-five as the dividing line under social security, and can well understand why the armed forces place it lower.

The task of an administrator is to decide, and the well-being of a large company in every phase of the business depends upon the crispness as well as the soundness of the decisions taken at each level. It isn't enough that they be wise; they must be forthright, prompt, and well-timed. Those are the attributes of youth, and each year as we pass middle life we possess them in lesser degree. Battles are won by generals in their forties, and most great surges of industrial expansion are conceived and carried through by men not yet fifty. For a time the older man merits responsibility because his growing wisdom, born of longer experience, offsets his diminishing audacity, but there comes a time when there is danger that his inertia with respect to decisions and the slower tempo of his mental processes will make him a bad risk in a deciding job. On the law of averages as I have observed men in the middle sixties, I still place the danger zone at age sixty-five. Because there is a risk, it is the duty of management to deal with it conservatively, and doubts on a subject such as this should be resolved in favor of the company instead of the individual.

But since all men are different, and individual characteristics vary widely in later years, why should not retirement be handled selectively, keeping those who are in their prime and releasing only those as to whom there is doubt? This is a plausible suggestion, often urged by those who have a particular man in mind who looks for all the world as good at sixty-five as he did at fifty. There are many such. Confidentially, I hope to be one myself. And the adherents of this theory believe it a serious thing for the nation that so much creative power is lost from the economy, and so much experience, at a time when the burdens of industry are so heavy and administrative capacity so scarce.

I think this is letting the heart rule the mind. There is first the difficulty that a man who seems fit today may be an altogether different person a year from now. We are talking of a time of life when changes come swiftly when they do come, with the man himself often the last to sense the change, and neither the doctors nor the psychologists have been able to establish standards by which significant changes may quickly be detected for men in key positions. Surely there comes a time when the risks of deterioration in the quality of leadership become too great for prudent management to accept, and the wise course is to erect a barrier and stay on the safe side of it. I place the barrier at sixty-five.

But if there were no other consideration involved there is one compelling reason why a fixed rule for retirement from deciding jobs is imperative, dealing with all alike, and that is the intolerable series of human repercussions that build up within a large organization when selectivity is undertaken. The whole integrity of the management may eventually be drawn in question as people take sides on the fairness of successive decisions. Suppose two vice-presidents are due for retirement in the same year, each with long years of service in the course of which they have made many friends all through the company. Management is fully satisfied with the work of one but would be relieved to have the other gone, and so retains the first but notifies the other that he will be expected to enter into retirement at his normal date. Dismay and anger rise in the heart of the second until he slams his desk shut and stalks out of the office never to return, telling his customers and old friends that never has a man been so shabbily treated. His former staff and associates take up the cudgels in his behalf, and watch the first man sharply from day to day, magnifying his faults to prove that actually he isn't half as good as their old boss, and saying that he should have been the first to go. Rumors start as to what it can be that the first man has on the boss to get such preferential treatment. Such tensions cannot be endured within a good company, and to invite them from year to year by a program of selectivity that rests at best upon discretion is not sound administration. As a contrast, if there is a rule and everybody knows that it is enforced, all concerned take retirement in their stride, and the farewell dinners reflect universal friendliness and good will.

But what a tragedy it is, both for the company and the man, when a once able chief executive of a large publicly owned company accepts no rule as to himself, and goes on toward the shadow of senility with no one to protect him from the consequences of his own folly. He himself is by hypothesis unaware of the failure of his powers, and at first only his intimates understand. Gradually, however, even the chance acquaintance begins to wonder and the whispering starts. He talks with the old volubility, and still uses a vivid diction, but at the end of a long discourse you realize that he has really said nothing, and you are heavyhearted for him. Instinctively he justifies his hanging on by keeping on likewise all of the other older men, and inexorably as the years drag on the pace of the whole organization slows down, and the brilliant leadership of the past is forgotten in the confusion of the present. Only a rule can prevent such catastrophes.

The saddest part of all for me, however, is the plight of the man who fights retirement for his own sake. "What will I do?" What a commentary on business as a career! "My office is a pretty comfortable place, and I'd be bored to death just sitting around the house. So would my wife." Are the stockholders conducting a social agency for the purpose of solving the inner frustrations of aging officials? "I have no hobby." How I hate that word! As though whittling would solve everything if more widely practiced as an art.

What has such a man been doing all his life? Has nothing challenged him except the daily routine? Has he no unfinished business in terms of the durable satisfactions of life; no dreams that have not come true for which there is still abundant time? Has he never lifted his eyes to the world about him and sensed the infinite variety of opportunity that awaits a man of proven

[172   ]

ability for service to his community? Actually, in these critical days when every ounce of energy and every scrap of wisdom could and should be harnessed for the good of our country, and of the world, where is there a comparable reserve of brains and character such as could be provided if every businessman upon retirement would volunteer his service on a full or part time basis, suited to his health, in some form of public activity? It is the pay-off time for the man who has enjoyed the fruits of free enterprise to repay society for extending to him that privilege.

In saying these things, I shall change the thinking of no man now worrying about retirement, but I address them particularly to the juniors who have not yet reached middle life. They are at the time in their careers when unconsciously they are preparing for retirement. If they live full lives now, entering richly into the activities of their communities and discovering areas of challenge totally unrelated to their jobs, they will be no problem to anyone when their turn comes for retirement. They will have much unfinished business.

CHAPTER XII The Business of
Thinking

As I LOOK BACK over what I have written, I am led to
wonder how it is that the opinion a man holds about
any particular subject comes into being. For the most
part the origins of an idea must be buried too deeply in
one's background of environment and education for
the faint beginnings to be discernible, but that is not
always true. Sometimes in a letter, during a business
conference, or even in a chance conversation on a
train you suddenly face up to a new problem, and if
while the mood is on you say or write something
apropos, you have formed an opinion. Chances are you
have locked yourself in on it, too, but from then on
you build on a foundation, the cornerstone for which
was laid at a particular time and place.

Good talk with keen minds is essential to the development of an orderly set of opinions, and that is
a working tool that is rather hard to come by in busi-

ness. The occasions on which we sit quietly with our feet up and our hair down exchanging observations with men like ourselves, and covering subjects other than the urgent one for which we may have come together, are not frequent. The pace is too hot, or so we think. I find it hard to remember when I have been invited to a small luncheon or dinner with business friends just for talk. And if I were, I suspect that the self-conscious host would soon fear that general boredom was about to set in, and suggest a game of bridge, or gin rummy.

Yet, saying things in private is the best possible preparation for saying them in public. When you try out a newly-formed opinion on a group of merciless friends, the fat gets trimmed off it in short order, and thereafter you feel much safer in exposing it to an audience who can't talk back. And each time you say it new implications develop in your mind, and you strengthen it by documentation that had escaped you earlier. As you shave in the morning, or drive to work in your car, this new idea that you have acquired keeps coming back to your mind, and you embroider it. You think of the answer you should have made to your friend who was so critical of it, and more and more you become convinced that you were right and that he was wrong. And thus opinion is formed. All that remains is to give it currency so that it may have a part in forming general opinion.

Good reading is as important as good talk, both as a corrective on tentative opinions already held, and by way of enticing one's mind to follow altogether new avenues of thought. But good reading is likewise hard to achieve in a busy life. The great mass of factual material that each of us must wade through in a day in order to keep abreast of what is going on in our field of primary responsibility leaves us at evening physically and mentally so weary that even the paper will drop from our hands as we nod. But some of our indifference to books is habit of mind. With our stylized recreation, and our effortless forms of entertainment, we may be losing some of the mental discipline required to be stimulated by a good book; but we must recapture that quality if as businessmen we are determined to re-establish leadership by the soundness of our opinions. That is one miracle that not even television can perform for us.

Above all we need the spirit of high adventure in our business thinking. This is a magnificent time in which to live. History is being made for all time. Vast ideas are on the march, and the air is heavy with excitement. Nothing has yet been decided with finality, and whoever wishes to strike a blow for the things he believes in may still enter the battle. In fact, the break may be at hand. This is no last-ditch struggle, no rear-guard action for free enterprise; actually the counter-charge may even now be forming which will deliver the final blow for our side.

As happy warriors, let us meet the challenge of socialism. Each man in his place, each voice lifted in confidence, each so living that none can fail to admire, let us cause our faith in free enterprise to come alive in the hearts of men everywhere by the compelling quality of our achievements for the common good.